THE COLLAPSE OF RICHMOND'S CHURCH HILL TUNNEL

THE COLLAPSE OF RICHMOND'S CHURCH HILL TUNNEL

WALTER S. GRIGGS JR.

THE History PRESS

Published by The History Press
Charleston, SC 29403
www.historypress.net

Front cover: Courtesy of the Chesapeake and Ohio Historical Society. *Back cover:* Courtesy of the Chesapeake and Ohio Historical Society and the Virginia Historical Society.

First published 2011

ISBN 978-1-5402-0611-4

Library of Congress CIP data applied for.

Notice: The information in this book is true and complete to the best of our knowledge. It is offered without guarantee on the part of the author or The History Press. The author and The History Press disclaim all liability in connection with the use of this book.

This book is dedicated to my wife, Frances Pitchford Griggs, who kept the story on track and kept grammatical errors from derailing it, and to my daughter, Cara Frances Griggs, whose skill as a research archivist led me to much of the information in this book. Just as my wife kept the grammar on track, my daughter helped me to find the tracks.

Contents

Preface 9
Acknowledgments 13
Introduction 15

1. The Genealogy of the Chesapeake and Ohio Railroad 19
2. Plans for the Church Hill Tunnel 26
3. The Challenge of Digging a Tunnel 30
4. The Construction of the Church Hill Tunnel 33
5. Trains under Church Hill 45
6. A Viaduct, a Station and a Three-Level Crossing 52
7. The Extension and Closing of the Church Hill Tunnel 58
8. The Tunnel Is Returned to Use 61
9. Friday, October 2, 1925 63
10. Saturday, October 3, 1925 80
11. Sunday, October 4, 1925 85
12. Monday, October 5, 1925 90
13. Tuesday, October 6, 1925 93
14. Wednesday, October 7, 1925 96
15. Thursday, October 8, 1925 98
16. Friday, October 9, 1925 99
17. Saturday, October 10, 1925 101

18. Sunday, October 11, 1925 103
19. Monday, October 12, 1925 105
20. Thursday, October 15, 1925 106
21. Friday, October 23, 1925 107
22. Remembering the Church Hill Tunnel 111

Bibliography 121
About the Author 127

Preface

My grandfather, Martin O. Feitig, owned a grocery store at Twenty-fifth and P Streets in Richmond's Church Hill. "Martin O. Feitig's Fancy Groceries: 'You pay me so I can pay others'" was painted on the side of the store. Frequently, he would take me along in his old orange delivery truck when he made grocery deliveries to his customers in the East End of Richmond. It must have been around 1945 that he turned down an unpaved road next to a large brick building and pointed out the sealed-off entry to an old tunnel. He then told me in a somewhat mysterious voice that there were dead men and a train buried in the tunnel. I recall being scared to death and very happy to leave the tunnel and the creepy, mysterious feelings it seemed to project.

When I arrived home, I could not get that old tunnel out of my mind. After I learned to drive, I would drive my Corvair to see it and wonder if a train and dead men were really behind that cold, concrete, weed-covered, water-stained wall with 1926 chiseled on it. Over time the old tunnel became an obsession with me. I could not get it out of my mind.

During my high school years, I listened to radio station WRVA for school closing information. In memory of the train in the Church Hill Tunnel, longtime announcer Alden Aaroe would always sound a steam whistle at 6:45 a.m. since the station was very close to the western portal of the tunnel.

My high school friend Donald Cornell got a job on the C&O, and I used to go to R Cabin in Fulton Yard to watch the trains. I would also try to figure out more about railroading and how the yard looked at a time when the Church Hill Tunnel was a part of the C&O.

As an undergraduate student at the University of Richmond, I used to watch a C&O diesel locomotive push coal cars to the university's power plant. Watching the locomotive push a hopper car was far more interesting to me than studying what the students called "Old Devil Math."

When I was a college senior majoring in history, I had to write a thesis to complete my graduation requirements, and I selected the Church Hill Tunnel. By doing research for my thesis, I hoped to learn the history of the tunnel. I used to sit on the steps of the abandoned Westham Station on the Chesapeake and Ohio Railway's James River Division and work on my thesis. When a train came along, I would take a picture of it with my Kodak Signet 80 camera.

In the course of my research on the tunnel, I learned that fireman Benjamin F. Mosby, who was in the locomotive when the tunnel caved in, died in Grace Hospital, the same hospital in which I was born and in which my grandmother died. I also learned that the tunnel's eastern portal was near Chimborazo Park. It was in this park that I used to play as a child and put caterpillars on sticks and watch them crawl around it.

During the course of my research, I talked to railroad men and spent many hours, in places where I should not have been, taking pictures. I also did research in the Richmond Public Library and the Virginia State Library, now the Library of Virginia. In those days, I had to make notes on three- by five-inch or four- by six-inch cards since there were no copy machines; and I looked at endless rolls of microfilm since there were no databases, computers or indexes. I do not recall who typed my thesis, but it was typed on a manual typewriter on which, when a bell rang, the typist had to push the paper carriage back. Since my thesis was typed in a world without spell check, computers or delete buttons, it was typed on state-of-the-art erasable paper so corrections could be made with ease. If the corrections were extensive, a bottle of Wite-Out was nearby. Although it is slowly falling apart, I still have my thesis with the grade of "A" barely visible—but it is still visible!

Even though I completed my thesis and went on to law school, I still could not get that tunnel out of my mind. I even kept an old railroad spike from the track leading into the tunnel on my desk to help me remember it. In the meantime, I continued to write stories about the tunnel for magazines and to make speeches on it to various organizations. I even took my future wife on a date to see the tunnel. Some date! After we were married and our daughter was born, I took many pictures of our daughter, Cara, standing in front of the tunnel. Now almost fifty years after I wrote my thesis, I have the privilege of writing a book covering the history of a tunnel that has been a part of my life since my grandfather first showed it to me so many years ago.

Acknowledgments

Since this book was written over a period of fifty years, many of the people who helped me have passed away, but their contributions will never be forgotten. Dr. Charles Turner of Washington and Lee University elaborated on some of the material in his book, *Chessie's Road.* I still recall his kindness to me. Mr. I.R. Rose, an engineer on the Chesapeake and Ohio Railway, offered some interesting speculation on the tunnel. Information on railroad operations came from K.A. "Mac" McManaway, an engineer on the Atlantic Coast Line Railroad and a man whom I will never forget. Ted O'Mera of the Chesapeake and Ohio furnished records on the replacement of the tunnel by the unique viaduct in 1901. Mrs. Kate Brown, who lived very close to the tunnel, told me stories of hearing the sounds of steam shovels and watching men dig shafts into Jefferson Park in a desperate effort to save those trapped in the tunnel. My mother, who was only nine years old when the tunnel caved in, still remembered people running into the street when the disaster at the tunnel became known; and my father and his family came from King and Queen County to watch the efforts to rescue those trapped in the tunnel. This writer is also indebted to all of the men of the C&O who were willing to share their recollections with me.

For their contributions to the book, I would like to thank Dr. Annie Stith-Willis for some very helpful conversations about the role of African Americans in the development of the South. I would like to thank the archives staff of the Library of Virginia, including my daughter, Cara F. Griggs, who was not around when I wrote my thesis but helped me to locate a lot of important information, as well as taking and editing most of the contemporary pictures in this book. Fortunately, she did see and hear a restored Southern Railway steam locomotive when she was very young. When its whistles screamed, she exclaimed, "It scared my ears!" Also at the Library of Virginia, I would like to express my appreciation to Chris Kolbe for his assistance in securing permission to use the maps in this book.

In addition, I want to thank the staff of the Virginia Historical Society, especially Frances Pollard and Jamison Davis for their assistance in securing pictures and giving me permission to use them in this book. The staff members of the Richmond Public Library and the Virginia Commonwealth University Library were also helpful to me in securing information and pictures. I would also like to thank all of my students at Virginia Commonwealth University who listened to my tunnel stories for forty years.

I want to thank Russell Lawson for permission to include his prize-winning song, "The Church Hill Tunnel," in this book and Jim Scott and Louis Salomonsky for their efforts in securing a state marker for the tunnel. I also want to recognize the support of the Railroad and Locomotive Historical Society and the Chesapeake and Ohio Railway Historical Society.

There are many other people who have encouraged and supported me in this effort: Bob and Sue Griggs, who once lived over a Great Northern Railroad yard and allowed me to take pictures out their apartment window; Jerry Becker, who is one of the few people who remember when I wrote my thesis; and the Mouse Lounge coffee crowd at VCU, including Jill Kramer (member emeritus), Linda Pontius, Marianne Miller, Pam Burch, Mike Tharp, Stephanie Kite and Glenn Gilbreath. Jason Chan at Virginia Commonwealth University kept my computer on life support, and Peggy Bullinger helped me to appreciate the hills of West Virginia. I am also grateful to Tom Silvestri and Robin Beres of the *Richmond Times-Dispatch*; Rebecca Benton of Ritz Camera Shop at Willow Lawn, who answered a lot of my questions about digital photography; and to Amber Allen and Jessica Berzon of The History Press, who made a dream come true.

Introduction

Millions of years ago, Richmond, Virginia, was covered with water. Even today, remains of prehistoric sea life can be found in the earth under the Church Hill section of Richmond. The waters receded long ago, but they were destined to play a major role in the history of the Chesapeake and Ohio Railway and the City of Richmond.

The area we call Richmond was once occupied by Native Americans who saw the settlers from Jamestown sail up the James River and place a cross at the future site of the city. In the course of time, Richmond was settled and became not only the capital of Virginia but also the capital of the Confederacy during the Civil War.

When the Confederate soldiers abandoned Richmond in April 1865, officers on worn-out horses and long, gray lines of infantrymen on foot trudged from the burning capital city to a little-known place called Appomattox Court House, Virginia. Many factors resulted in the defeat of the Confederacy, including lack of food, lack of soldiers, the overpowering strength of the Union army and the broken and twisted railroad tracks over which the soldiers stumbled as they headed west. These broken rails reflected the fires from hundreds of burning buildings, as the last of the Confederate soldiers left Richmond and became silhouetted against a blazing April sky.

Richmond, after the fall of the Confederate nation, became well acquainted with the rigors and humiliations of military reconstruction. The once proud city was now patrolled by soldiers in blue uniforms, and

Virginia now suffered the indignity of being called Military District no. 1. Yet because of, or in spite of, the terrible times of Reconstruction, the city began to rebuild itself. New buildings rose upon the charred foundations of burned-out structures. Flowers reappeared in trampled gardens, and the chirping of birds was no longer drowned out by the thunderous sounds of distant cannon fire. And there were also the sounds of railroad spikes being pounded into crossties, as broken tracks were repaired or replaced. Soon locomotives began to pull trains on tracks radiating out from Richmond, as Richmond emerged from a city of despair to a city with a vision of recovery.

On February 1, 1872, an important link in this rebuilding process occurred when ground was broken for a railroad tunnel under Richmond's Church Hill. Beginning near Shockoe Creek in the vicinity of Nineteenth Street, the tunnel was dug under Jefferson Park, crossed under Broad Street, passed near St. John's Church where Patrick Henry proclaimed, "Give me liberty, or give me death" and came out below Chimborazo Park, which only a few years earlier had been the site of the largest military hospital in America. From portal to portal, the tunnel stretched almost four thousand feet under historic Church Hill. The construction of the tunnel was a source of pride to Richmonders; but during its construction, it had numerous cave-ins that cost a number of workers their lives.

After it was completed, the tunnel enabled train traffic to go from the docks on the James River to the C&O railroad yards at Seventeenth Street. But Richmond's future as a port city was short-lived. When tracks were laid to the deep water ports in Tidewater, Virginia, along with the construction of a new viaduct in Richmond, the tunnel soon fell into disuse, and for a number of years, it was rarely used. But as rail traffic increased on the C&O, the decision was made to restore the tunnel and return it to use. This decision would prove to be a mistake.

On October 2, 1925, Chesapeake and Ohio locomotive no. 231 entered the tunnel, pulling flatcars to aid in the reopening of the tunnel. The train had almost reached the western portal near Eighteenth Street when bricks fell from the tunnel's ceiling, the earth caved in and several railroad workers were trapped and died. Following the cave-in, there were heroic efforts to save the trapped men, but the efforts failed, and at least two men remain buried in the tunnel along with the locomotive that, in the words of a song, "Will Never Return." In 1926, the Church Hill Tunnel was sealed off and became a tomb for both the men and the locomotive.

Inscription on the west portal, indicating the time that it was sealed. *Photograph by Walter Griggs.*

Today, people can stand at the western portal of the tunnel and recall its history as both a tunnel and a tomb. In addition, urban legends have developed around the tunnel. Its mystery will continue as long as there are those who have a passion to study the past and the lurking ghosts and vampires of the present.

Chapter 1

The Genealogy of the Chesapeake and Ohio Railroad

Trains cross the continent in a swirl of dust and thunder; the leaves fly down the tracks behind them; the great trains cleave through gulch and gully, they rumble with spiked thunder on the bridges over the brown wash of mighty rivers, they toil through hills, they skirt the rough brown stubble of shorn fields, they whip past the empty stations in the little towns and their great stride pounds its even pulse across America.
—*Thomas Wolfe,* Of Time and the River

Virginians are passionate about tracing their family history back to at least Jamestown, Virginia, if not to Adam and Eve. The Library of Virginia, the Virginia Historical Society and other repositories of archival material are filled with people hunched over old papers, wills, books covered with "red rot" and family Bibles, trying to trace their families back as far as possible and to prove that they are related in some way to a distinguished person who fought with George Washington or Robert E. Lee or signed some important document like the Declaration of Independence. It seems that the study of genealogy is a passion for many Virginians, in general, and Richmonders, in particular.

Like families, railroads have family trees that frequently explain their origins, mergers, development, accomplishments, failures and ongoing challenges. For example, the Union Pacific can claim to be a part of the first transcontinental railroad that crossed the United States, and the Southern Pacific has as one of its ancestors the Central Pacific, which was also a part of the first transcontinental railroad. The Baltimore and Ohio can claim to be one of the first railroads to be built in the United States, and the Alaska Railroad is known for having to chase moose off of its tracks with a device called a "moose-gooser."

The C&O is no exception, but it has a family lineage that can be termed truly aristocratic and includes up to 150 railroads that were added to its family tree over the years. Its genealogical history would make anyone proud—even a Virginian.

The history of the C&O has two distinguished branches. The oldest branch can be traced back to the James River and Kanawha Canal Company that began in the 1780s and was supported by George Washington. The canal was planned as a means of providing transportation to the west by connecting the James River in eastern Virginia to the Kanawha River in western Virginia, now West Virginia. The Kanawha River was the objective since it flows into the Ohio River and opens the Ohio and Mississippi Rivers to the cities on the eastern seaboard.

When the canal was opened from Richmond to Lynchburg in 1840, there was a big celebration. The orator at the opening dedication in Lynchburg rose to such heights during his speech that he fell into the canal. As the canal inched westward, picturesque packet boats filled with passengers, accompanied by bateaus loaded with tobacco, were pulled by mules or horses walking on the tow path next to the canal. For the true romantic, the canalboats reminded them of the gondolas of Venice, Italy.

Although the James River and Kanawha Canal Company was designed to reach the Kanawha River in western Virginia, it only reached the town of Buchanan in Botetourt County, Virginia, which is about 150 miles west of Richmond. It was never completed to the Kanawha River.

The genealogical linkage between George Washington and the Chesapeake and Ohio exists because the Richmond and Alleghany Railroad Company laid railroad tracks along the towpath of the old canal. Eventually, the Richmond and Alleghany Railroad Company reached from Richmond to Clifton Forge, Virginia. It could be said that the iron horses replaced the mules and horses as the pulling power along the towpath. In 1889, the Richmond and Allegany Railroad was acquired by the Chesapeake and Ohio, thus establishing a genealogical link with George Washington. This connection was worthy of an FFV (First Families of Virginia). Indeed, the

C&O had been referred to as George Washington's Railroad; in the years ahead, the railroad would name a passenger train in honor of the first president of the United States.

The second link in the corporate family ancestry of the Chesapeake and Ohio was a railroad and not a canal. Railroads replaced the canals as a more versatile means of transportation, and they were better able to meet the needs of Virginians. As a practical matter, railroads were cheaper than canals and usually took less time to reach a desired destination.

The Louisa Railroad Company was destined to become the railroad ancestor of the C&O. This railroad was chartered by the Commonwealth of Virginia in 1836 and began to operate in 1837. Like most southern railroads built prior to the Civil War, the Louisa Railroad was probably built by slave labor. When the railroad was completed, there was a celebration. A locomotive and three cars departed Richmond on the tracks of the Richmond, Fredericksburg and Potomac Railroad and then switched to the new Louisa Railroad tracks. Decorated with flags, the train was pulled by a locomotive that burned cordwood and bellowed smoke from its massive smokestack. On board were distinguished guests, including Virginia's lieutenant governor, William F. McFarland, who was the chief speaker of the day. Although there was a big celebration, the railroad was only twenty-one miles long, but it was the start of what would become the Chesapeake and Ohio Railroad.

The Louisa Railroad carried passengers, farm produce and lumber, as well as other products. To expand its service area, the Louisa Railroad continued to lay more track, and by the 1850s, the railroad had been completed between Charlottesville and Richmond. No longer a railroad just serving the transportation needs of Louisa County, it was renamed the Virginia Central Railroad to reflect its expanding service area. It was said that the motto of the railroad was "Westward Ho" because its ultimate goal was to lay rails to the Ohio River. Indeed, two of its early locomotives were named Westward Ho, and one of them was used in the Civil War.

As the tracks of the Virginia Central and other railroads continued to spread across Virginia, the Civil War was looming on the horizon. When Confederate cannonballs fell on Fort Sumter and the Stars and Stripes were hauled down and replaced by the Stars and Bars, Virginia joined the Confederacy and became a battleground.

The Virginia Central served the Confederacy by carrying troops and supplies, and on a few occasions, it brought soldiers directly to the battlefield where they were immediately deployed. But the Virginia Central paid a heavy price for its service to the Confederate nation. Because railroads were a prime military objective, the Virginia Central was virtually destroyed by Union forces in keeping with Union general George Gordon Mead's belief: "Until that road [Virginia Central] is destroyed we cannot compel the evacuation of Richmond." And the railroad was almost destroyed. A report in the *Richmond Dispatch* stated:

> *The Virginia Central was literally wrecked. Its rolling stock and rails were worn to a frazzle; its roadbed was the prey of raiders; its bridges were frequently held together only by providential interposition; and the expedients resorted to by its engineers and mechanics to keep it going were as ingenious as they were numerous.*

By war's end, it had only about five miles of track still in operation and about forty dollars in gold in its treasury.

Following the surrender of General Robert E. Lee at Appomattox Court House, Virginia, in April 1865, the state legislatures of both Virginia and the newly created state of West Virginia enacted laws to provide for the completion of a rail system linking the waters of the Chesapeake Bay to the Ohio River.

The legislation was as follows:

> *The Virginia Central Railroad Company may contract with the Covington and Ohio Railroad commissioners for the construction of the railroad from Covington,* [Virginia,] *to the Ohio River; and in the event such a contract is made, the said Virginia Central Railroad Company shall be known as The Chesapeake and Ohio Railroad Company.*

On August 31, 1868, in keeping with the enabling legislation, the Virginia Central merged with the Covington and Ohio, and the Chesapeake and Ohio Railroad was created. The stage was now set to connect the waters of the Atlantic Ocean with the flowing waters of the Ohio River.

With the corporate structure of the railroad in place, the next challenge was to acquire financing for the expansion of the C&O. The leadership of the railroad turned to Great Britain for financial support, but it was not forthcoming. Fortunately, funds became available from the North, the same area of the nation whose armies had destroyed the Southern railroads. Collis P. Huntington of New York believed that the Chesapeake and Ohio might provide an important link in his envisioned coast-to-coast chain of railroads. Huntington's involvement was extremely fortunate.

Born in Connecticut in 1821, Huntington left home at an early age and became a farmer and a storekeeper. Moving to California, he opened a successful store, became heavily involved in the Republican Party and helped to finance the Central Pacific Railroad. With railroads, he found his passion and was one of the men responsible for the first transcontinental railroad across the United States. With a record of accomplishments, Huntington now supplied the funds to lay the tracks of the C&O to the Ohio River.

Just as George Washington was a proponent of the canal, General Robert E. Lee supported railroad construction. In a letter written from Lexington, Virginia, dated September 21, 1868, the general wrote, "I am greatly pleased to learn of the execution of the contract for the completion of the Covington and Ohio Railroad and the formation of the Chesapeake and Ohio Railroad for the extension of the road to the Ohio River." The general believed the railroad would bring the products of the west to the eastern seaboard. He concluded that the Chesapeake and Ohio Railroad had the advantage "over the northern routes in distance, in grade, and freedom from interruption by severity of climate." General Lee also commented, "That no work of internal improvement, within my knowledge...excites greater interest in this favor, or promises to be more useful when completed." Joining Lee in support of the railroad was Matthew Fontaine Maury, who was well known as the "Pathfinder of the Seas." Maury wrote in 1868, "There seems to me to be no room for difference of opinion as to the merits of the Chesapeake and Ohio." Two iconic figures were firmly in support of the proposed railroad expansion, and Collis P. Huntington's financial resources made the dreams of both Lee and Maury become a reality. But it took the backbreaking labor of some very strong men to lay the tracks through the West Virginia mountains.

Laying track is always a challenge, and the route of the Chesapeake and Ohio through the Allegheny Mountains made a difficult job even harder. Although these mountains might have been "almost heaven" for John Denver, they must have been almost hell for those who had to lay the tracks through them. It is a tribute to human will that men can lay tracks around mountains, through valleys and across rivers to link cities together with ribbons of steel.

The lives of these pioneer railroad men were filled with both adventure and danger. One mistake, one false step, one missed hammer blow, one broken ax handle or one hungry bear could cause serious injury or death. History does not record the names of most of those men, but the men who laid the tracks on ties of wood and heard the blowing of the lonesome whistle were as important to the railroad as surveyors, engineers and financiers.

Finally, in 1873, the Chesapeake and Ohio Railroad's name had been fulfilled by linking Tidewater, Virginia, with the "Western Waters" of the Ohio River. As the rails went west, ceremonies were held along the C&O's mainline when a train entered a town for the first time following a trip from Richmond. The *Charleston Courier* of January 28, 1873, reported:

> *The arrival of this first train from Richmond will be welcomed at Huntington with a salute of one hundred guns, surely our metropolis* [Charleston] *can afford to rake up some old ordinance and give them a passing salute. Let the city fathers look to it that our city shall not be behind our "country cousin" Huntington.*

Then there was the welcome at Huntington. The *Richmond Whig* of February 3, 1873, proclaimed the completion of the line from Richmond to Huntington, West Virginia:

> *Punctual to the hour, the headlight of the engine appeared around the bend and she rushed screaming into our town* [Huntington]. *The first train from Richmond to Huntington had arrived. To say that the occupants of that train were welcomed would be a feeble way of expressing the enthusiastic display. A yell burst forth as they came up to the platform and the passengers were almost dragged out by eager hands.*

Another part of the arrival ceremony was symbolic. A demijohn of water from the Atlantic Ocean was poured into the Ohio River. Now the two bodies of water flowed together, symbolizing the connection of the eastern ocean with a western river.

And there were celebrations in Richmond. The first freight train from West Virginia to Richmond was expected to reach Richmond on February 12, 1873. An immense crowd gathered at the station, but the train did not arrive; it had been delayed by a landslide. Arriving the next day, it pulled only four cars of coal. These cars had been separated from the rest of the train, and the remainder of the cars was still blocked by the landslide. In spite of the delay, thousands of people gathered to see the train arrive. Businesses were closed, cannons were fired, bells were rung and factory whistles blew. It was a great day because railroad connections from the west to the east were established. There is some evidence that water from the Ohio River was brought to Richmond on the train and poured into the James River to show the completion of the rail from the west to the east. Although completing the rail line was very good news, it was tempered when the financial panic of 1873 occurred. The years ahead for the C&O would be difficult.

With the goal of reaching the Ohio River completed, Huntington next planned to further expand the C&O both to the west and to the east. Included in his plan was an expansion eastward from Richmond because a connection with Tidewater and its Atlantic Ocean ports was essential to the success of the railroad. This plan established the need for a way to get rail traffic through, around, over or even under Richmond.

The problem confronting the C&O's Richmond operation was that Richmond, like ancient Rome, had been built on many hills. Because of the many changes in the urban landscape since the 1870s, it is difficult for people today to appreciate the challenges these hills made for the C&O.

But when someone drives on Broad Street starting around Seventeenth Street and continues on Broad Street until it becomes Government Road and then to the intersection with the railroad tracks on Government Road, they become aware that they are going up or down a hill. Known as Church Hill, this hill was a nemesis for the C&O. In planning to lay tracks and expand the C&O to the east, it was necessary to determine how to get a train across Church Hill. To accomplish this task would prove to be a major challenge for the C&O.

Chapter 2

Plans for the Church Hill Tunnel

I've been workin' on the railroad,
All the live long day.
I've been workin' on the railroad,
Just to pass the time away
Don't you hear the whistle blowing?
Rise up so early in the morn.
Don't you hear the captain shouting
"Dinah, blow your horn?"
—Unknown, "I've Been Working on the Railroad"

Across the years, people and commerce have moved along trails, paths, roads, canals and then railroads. Railroads quickly proved to be superior to any other means of transportation, and by the 1840s, a clear link had been established between access to railroads and the urban growth and development of a city. United States senator Charles Sumner observed, "Where railroads are not, civilization cannot be. Under God, the railroad and the schoolmaster are the two chief agents of human improvement." Essentially, those cities with railroads prospered, and those that lacked railroads faded. It seemed to be that simple. Richmond was served by many railroads that enabled the city to prosper, but these railroads were frequently criticized because of the nuisance of having railroad tracks in the streets that caused traffic problems, bellowing smoke from steam engines that polluted downtown Richmond and shabby stations that were viewed as blights on the urban landscape.

But these criticisms were minor when weighed against the real and perceived benefits of the railroads. Richmond knew it needed the railroads if it was going to prosper; therefore, the city leaders were willing to listen to Collis P. Huntington explain the problem with the C&O's Richmond operation. He presented it this way:

> *The lack of tracks to the docks* [at Richmond] *near Fulton results in a charge for cartage and extra handling accrues…on all freight destined for transshipment. It is presumed that the citizens of Richmond are sensible of the importance of having this restriction upon its commerce speedily removed, and they will…propose to the Chesapeake and Ohio such right of way and other facilities for extending its tracks to the water-line.*

Two alternative routes were suggested by H.D. Whitcomb, the chief engineer of the C&O Railroad, for the connection to the James River. One plan was to connect the present depot grounds at Seventeenth Street with the docks on the James River by means of a tunnel under Church Hill. The other plan was to construct a branch track, leaving the mainline one mile from the city and passing over the hill to a point below Rocketts Landing. Rocketts was named for Robert Rocketts, who operated a ferry that was located on the James River in the vicinity of the C&O's Fulton Yard. Although the railroad tracks across Church Hill were less expensive, they would put more trains on the city streets, which was already a problem, and it would disrupt many businesses. Therefore, the tunnel option was finally selected because it interfered less with the streets of the city, it furnished a better rail line for business and it was above the highest flood level ever known on the James River. Indeed, there was an expectation that the tunnel would be an "opening to wealth and fortune: to many Richmonders." A reporter commented, "The tunnel would be promoted by the city to help the down-towners, the up-towners, and all other sections of Richmond."

With the selection of the tunnel option, Collis P. Huntington next made his case for financial assistance to the City of Richmond to build the proposed tunnel to connect the railroad yards on Seventeenth Street to the docks on the James River. Such requests for funding to a city or state by railroad officials were quite common. The City of Richmond saw the benefits in this project and responded to Huntington's request for financial assistance with an appropriation of $200,000 made on November 16, 1871. The president of the Richmond Chamber of Commerce asserted the rationale for the funding by saying, "[I want Richmond] to be treated as a terminus and not as a way station." The Church Hill Tunnel was viewed as a way to make Richmond a terminus.

The initial appropriation for the funding of the tunnel was repealed on December 23 of the same year and replaced with the following ordinance:

> *The Council of the City of Richmond hereby offers and proposes to contract, on behalf of the city, with the Chesapeake and Ohio Railroad Company for the connection of the said railroad with Tidewater in and near the city, according to the plan and upon the terms following—viz.*
>
> *1. The Chesapeake and Ohio Railroad Company*...[can] *construct a tunnel under Nineteenth Street and all intervening streets to near Twenty-ninth Street, between Broad and Grace; then by open cutting or embankment...passing over the Richmond and York River railroad...and thence, by any practical routes to the river front.*
>
> *2. To aid in the construction of the work, and to secure to the city the trade facilities to result therefrom, the city will pay to the said Chesapeake and Ohio Railroad Company three hundred thousand dollars.*

The C&O was also advised that the James River would be dredged to eighteen and a half feet of water at high tide from the wharves of Rocketts to Hampton Roads. This promise to deepen the James River would be of major significance in the years ahead.

On December 29, 1871, the C&O accepted the offer of the City of Richmond and the dream of a Church Hill Tunnel became feasible.

On January 1, 1872, a document was prepared in the office of the Chesapeake and Ohio in Richmond that contained several provisions concerning the tunnel, including the following:

> *1. The tunnel through Church Hill will be worked from the approaches from a depression between Twenty-first and Twenty-Second Streets, and from a shaft between the eastern portal and Twenty-Second Street. A shaft*

will be sunk at the eastern portal also in order to work the tunnel from the approach cut is contemplated. Near the western portal and for a short distance near Twenty-first Street, an open cut may be made and the line of the original surface restored under the arching is completed.

2. The timber used for support must be white oak or other durable wood of suitable strength to resist crushing.

3. The lining of the tunnel with masonry must progress as rapidly as the excavation.

4. Provisions must be made so that trains of the usual dimensions can pass through the tunnel. The Company will, however, arrange the trains so as to hinder the work as little as the interests of the Railroad Company will permit.

The document was signed by H. D. Whitcomb, chief engineer of the Chesapeake and Ohio Railroad. Mr. Whitcomb was a genial, courteous gentleman and an outstanding civil engineer. Although born in Portland, Maine, he obtained deep roots in Virginia when he married a woman from Virginia and supported the Southern Confederacy.

With the plans and funding in place, the following notice was published: "The C&O Railroad invited proposals for building a double track tunnel under Church Hill with a view to building a depot at Rocketts on the James River. The City Council of Richmond has voted $300,000.00 in city bonds to the company for this purpose."

The proposal was on record. Everything was in place to construct a tunnel. Everyone was optimistic. But a glimpse into the future would show that the C&O was about to encounter problems that had existed since the dawn of time and would not be easily overcome.

Chapter 3

The Challenge of Digging a Tunnel

And God created great whales, and every living creature that moveth, which the waters brought forth abundantly.
—Genesis 1:21

The funding for the tunnel and the permission to build it would prove to be the easiest part of the construction process; much more difficult would be the digging of the tunnel under the historic Church Hill section of Richmond. Although the average Richmonder did not know it, the intended route of the tunnel would take it through the very unstable soil under Church Hill—soil that had been under water in prehistoric times.

Using the information that was available at the time of the construction, the engineers knew that the area to be tunneled through consisted of first, a stratum of ordinary red clay about fifteen feet deep from the surface; second, a bed of sand and gravel, a few feet in thickness and containing water; and the third layer, the main body of the hill, was composed of Miocene clay, containing innumerable microscopic skulls and many bones of marine animals; the bottom, or fourth, layer was probably granite.

When construction began on the tunnel, "large quantities of bones and teeth were found, not interposed in the material but generally in pockets." One scientist wrote that the digging "brought to light thousands of fossil remains of the gigantic marine monsters that, long years ago, swam in the deep ocean over the spot where [Richmond] now stands." A science journal edited by Jedediah Hotchkiss, who was the chief topographical engineer for General Thomas J. "Stonewall" Jackson, reported: "The workmen, observing the interest manifested at the finding of the deposit and the anxiety to secure every relic, conceived them to have a money value and did not fail to appropriate all the fine specimens." It is indeed unfortunate that more of these specimens, which were fish remains, were not retained to be studied by future generations. But the job of the laborers was to dig a tunnel and not to collect specimens from an ancient sea and give them to scientists to study.

Like the laborers, the tunnel engineers would have little time to reflect on the scientific value of ancient remains. The engineers now had to make a major decision before the tunnel could be constructed. They had to decide which method would be used to construct the tunnel.

There were several options available, with some dating back to tunnel construction techniques used by the ancient Romans; however, the C&O had developed a preference for the American System, or Block System, which was probably first used on the Oxford or Van Nest Gap Tunnel of the Delaware, Lackawanna and Western Railroad. The block system is defined

East portal of the Church Hill Tunnel in 1963 when it was used to transfer trains from the Southern Railway to the Chesapeake and Ohio Railway. *Photograph by Walter Griggs.*

as follows: "Block timbering is cross or rafter timbering, where, instead of three pieces consisting of a cap and two legs, the pieces are multiplied to five or nine wooden voussoirs [wedge shaped stones forming the curved part of an arch]." When this system was first used by the Delaware and Lackawanna in New Jersey in 1854, it was a success. The C&O adopted this system in 1860 and used it successfully in digging the Red Hill or "Mud" Tunnel. As one of the first railroads to use the block system, the C&O had experience in how to use it to build a tunnel and decided to use it to construct the Church Hill Tunnel. Henry Drinker, a tunnel expert, noted that the Church Hill Tunnel was exceptional as to the employment of block-arching in such soft ground. In fact, there were very few soft-ground tunnels in the United States. Generally, the block system is applied in loose rock, where the pressure to be met is from above rather than at the sides. In summary, the Church Hill Tunnel was going to be built using a method of tunnel construction that was not normally used in tunneling through soft ground. This decision would prove to be a major mistake.

Although the supervisors made all of the decisions, the process of construction was to be undertaken by men who were largely ignorant of the challenges and dangers that they were about to face. They did not know what might happen to them with the removal of every shovel full of the cold wet dirt. They would soon find out.

Chapter 4

The Construction of the Church Hill Tunnel

Safety is of the first importance in the discharge of duty.
—The Chesapeake and Ohio Railway Company Rule Book

February 1, 1872, was a significant day in the history of both Richmond and the Chesapeake and Ohio Railroad. Less than a decade after the burning of Richmond "about fifty white men and a good many Negroes assembled at the foot of Doin's Hill on 19th Street…to watch the first lick struck upon the Church Hill Tunnel by the Chesapeake and Ohio Railroad. The crowd included…men who were in search of a job as workers in the tunnel, as well as interested onlookers."

E.D. Taylor of the firm of R.W. Powers and Company was given the honor of breaking the ground to start the construction project. It was observed that "he succeeded in dislodging a few handfuls of the frozen dirt and then very cheerfully resigned the tools to more experienced workmen." The *Daily State Journal* added to the opening ceremony by stating that the ground was very hard and that Mr. Taylor was able to throw only a cup full of dirt before giving up. When jokingly asked how much he would charge to continue digging, Mr. Taylor responded, "About $5.00 a day." His offer was not accepted because the contractor could hire better workmen for less money. Haggerty and Brannon, the tunnel contractors, began work immediately after the ceremony. Some fifty men and thirty dump cars were initially employed in digging the tunnel, and more men and equipment would be added in the weeks to come.

Many of the black men who were watching the ceremony secured immediate employment in digging the tunnel. Some of these men were former slaves who would now be supervised by former Confederate officers and soldiers. Railroad work was attractive employment for black men since it was considered the best alternative to sharecropping or domestic service. In fact, numerous scholars have asserted that railroads were the most important industry for black men since the pay was good and the jobs tended to be steady.

The first loads of dirt removed from the tunnel were dumped on a lot near Lumpkin's Jail on Shockoe Creek. Prior to the Civil War, Lumpkin's Jail held slaves and was close to the western portal of the tunnel. Working with the contractors were H.D. Whitcomb, chief engineer of the C&O, and Channing M. Bolton, division engineer, who was in charge of the project.

Unlike Whitcomb, who was a Virginian by marriage, Bolton was born in Richmond in 1843. He was a graduate of the University of Virginia and was an engineer in the Confederate army. He helped to design the defenses around Richmond and was in most of the major Civil War battles, including the Battle of Gettysburg.

These two men and their associates were responsible for constructing a double-track tunnel three-fourths of a mile long at a maximum depth of about 115 feet through the soft treacherous soil of Church Hill. In the months ahead, many days would be uneventful, but there would also be days when the engineers and the laborers would encounter major problems. At a time in the history of construction when safety concerns were few and good judgment was not always practiced, many workers would be injured in cruel and grotesque ways, and lives would be lost.

Common laborers working in the Church Hill Tunnel were paid $1.00 to $1.50 per day; miners, $1.50 to $1.60; bricklayers, $3.50 to $4.00; and stonecutters, $3.00 to $4.00.

During the hiring process, the Church Hill neighborhood became concerned when they heard a rumor that convict labor was going to be used to dig the tunnel. The contractors emphatically denied the rumor and said that they "preferred to employ free labor." To find additional free laborers, the contractors ran the following add in the local newspapers: "Wanted-Railroad hands, to work both on the inside of the Church Hill Tunnel and outside work. Wages good, and payments made every two weeks. Apply at

Construction scene at the east portal of the Church Hill Tunnel in 1872. *Photograph courtesy of the Chesapeake and Ohio Railroad Historical Society.*

Contractor's Office, No. 2412 Broad Street, between Twenty-fourth and Twenty-fifth."

Mechanical aids in the construction of the tunnel included dump cars that were filled with material removed from the tunnel, pulled outside and dumped. These dump cars ran on rails and were moved by men, horses or steam power. Also used in the construction process were steam derricks, one of which was used at the eastern portal of the tunnel near Chimborazo Park. Although mechanical aids certainly helped, it was strong men, using picks and shovels, who dug a tunnel through the treacherous ground under Church Hill—ground that had never been touched by mortal man but had been soaked by an ancient sea.

Digging took place at the two tunnel portals near Seventeenth Street, which was known as the western portal, and Chimborazo Park, which was near the eastern portal. In addition, three shafts were sunk on the line of the tunnel to facilitate construction. The deepest of these shafts was in the area of Twenty-fourth and Broad Streets. When dirt was removed during the excavation of the tunnel, the excavated material was hauled up one of the shafts by a horse gin, which was a primitive device using horses to lift buckets filled with material taken from the tunnel. Later, steam power replaced the horses to provide additional power to remove the dirt. Dirt and debris from the tunnel was used to fill a deep gully that ran through Church Hill. When the gully was filled it became Church Hill Avenue, but it is now known as Jefferson Avenue.

Within a few months, the tunnel started to claim its victims. On May 25, 1872, around 1:00 p.m., there was a fatal accident in the tunnel. Mr. James M. Bolton, the assistant engineer in charge of the work, was killed. The *Richmond Dispatch* reported on the tragedy:

> *James Bolton was at Shaft No. 2 personally superintending and directing the operations in which he was so deeply interested when a huge piece of earth fell without warning from the roof of the excavation and struck him to the ground. He fell forward upon his face and, when picked up, was found to be internally injured and in a great deal of pain. Several physicians rushed to his aid, but after clinging to life for five hours, he died with many of his friends around him. Mr. Bolton was a popular man with a good mind and a religious disposition. His many friends had predicted for him a brilliant career, and indeed, he had already entered upon such a career. In the discharge of his duties, he met his death.*

Mr. Bolton's funeral took place at Monumental Church, which was built as a memorial to those who perished in the Richmond Theater Fire of 1811.

Following the tragic death of Mr. Bolton, a labor problem developed. About fifty black laborers struck for higher pay. Their pay was only $1.25 per day, and they demanded $1.75 per day. It was also noted that they were not paid on a regular basis.

But there were successes that were celebrated. In September 1872, the workers in Shafts no. 1 and 2 had "a subterranean meeting and a hearty handshake." They also took a social drink in commemoration of the progress they were making on the tunnel.

But celebrations were few and tragedies were many. It seemed that the earth was determined to stop the invasion by the tunnel and that an angel of death was commissioned to lead the fight and claim victims.

In December 1872, "Charles Owens, a young laborer in the tunnel, had a fatal accident at Shaft No. 3 at the corner of Grace and Twenty-ninth

Streets. Mr. Owen, who was very nearsighted, got out on the wrong side of a bucket used to bring dirt to the surface and fell 90 feet to his death." The *Daily State Journal* reported: "When his body was recovered, his life was entirely extinct."

In addition to accidents within the tunnel, there were numerous cave-ins. Church Hill residents and tunnel workers had learned that the first sign of an impending cave-in was generally the appearance of cracks in the earth's surface or the beginning of water dripping from the tunnel's roof. One of the most serious collapses occurred on January 13, 1873, in the area of Twenty-fourth and Broad Streets. The residents had been concerned about the area prior to the actual cave-in; however, no notice was taken of the cracks that started to appear over the tunnel. But when the tunnel contractors and the citizens saw how wide the cracks were getting, things got serious. The rector of St. John's Episcopal Church, the Reverend Dr. Henry Wall, and other residents in the Twenty-fourth Street area were advised to move their families out of the area. The families left just before the earth began sinking and breaking gas lines. The escaping gas from the broken lines caught fire, causing flames to shoot into the air. The local paper described the cave-in as "something like an earthquake."

The earthquake-like cave-in began around 9:00 a.m. on January 14, 1873, when a piece of ground about 120 feet long by 30 feet wide, partly on Twenty-fourth Street and partly on private property, sank 20 feet, carrying with it several just vacated houses. The piece of ground fell in one large piece, leaving the surface a pit with vertical ends and nearly vertical sides. When the tunnel caved in, there were seven workmen under the place where the earth collapsed. Fortunately, they heard the timbers holding the tunnel in place start to "crack, making sounds like muskets," and they crawled up the shaft at Twenty-ninth Street and escaped unharmed. These workmen reported that when the cave-in occurred, "There was wind so great that it was scarcely possible to maintain an erect position." Years later, another generation of workmen would feel a similar burst of wind. Several houses were either damaged or destroyed by the great tunnel collapse. The study and the kitchen of the rectory at St. John's Church collapsed into the hole in the ground. Ironically, The Reverend Dr. Wall's sermon on the Sunday before the collapse was on the text: "set your house in order." The newspaper reported that the "family of William B. Robins was at breakfast at the time and were warned of their danger by the breaking loose of the plastering above their heads." The family escaped just in time. One house turned a somersault, as it fell into the hole and ended its plunge resting on its side. Another house was smashed beyond recognition. Houses that were rendered unsafe by the cave-in flew the smallpox flag to warn people that the area was unsafe. In a humorous vein, the paper reported that everyone seemed to agree that there had never been such "a fall in Richmond's real estate."

The gaping hole on Broad Street became a major attraction for the curious. Police officers had to patrol the area to keep unwary visitors from falling into the hole. It was reported that "hundreds of ladies, many of whom went over Shockoe Hill in carriages, toured the site."

Although the engineers declared the tunnel safe following the cave-in, the congregation of Third Presbyterian Church, which was across Broad Street from St. John's Church, was not confident of its safety since the church was almost on top of the tunnel. To alleviate the concern of the church members, additional supports were placed under the church. But the congregation was still worried about the safety of their brick church, so they moved across the street and held services at St. John's Episcopal Church. A new Presbyterian church was eventually built nearby and dedicated in 1876. The site of the old church is now a park.

While the curious looked at the cave-in and gaped in wonderment, the people whose homes were destroyed were desperate for help. The Chesapeake and Ohio officials responded to those who were displaced. They secured homes for those left homeless and did everything possible to assist them with the loss of their property and possessions. The local newspapers complimented the railroad on the prompt response to help those affected by the cave-in.

The cave-in was a major setback, but it did not stop the work on the tunnel. If it was a warning of things to come, it was ignored. To clean out the debris that blocked the tunnel, a fourth shaft had to be dug. The railroad bought a vacant lot on the southeast corner of Broad and Twenty-sixth Streets as the site for the new shaft. It took weeks for the tunnel to be cleared of the dirt from the cave-in and for the digging of the tunnel to resume.

Why did the cave-in happen? The media reported that some supports had been removed from the area of the cave-in. Henry Drinker concluded, "The tunnel caved in during an attempt to move some of the supporting timbers preparatory to arching the tunnel with masonry." He continued, "If the system of timbering had been thoroughly tied longitudinally (lengthwise)... the accident would not have happened."

This cave-in was large and could be seen by onlookers. But there were many accidents and small cave-ins that occurred underground that were not seen by the general public. On January 26, 1873, George Dorsett, a tunnel watchman, fell down Shaft no.1 and was killed. It was presumed that the steam, smoke and vapor that enveloped everything about the shaft obscured the shaft from view, made it impossible for him to see it and resulted in his death. A few weeks later, Edward Foster was killed near Shaft no. 3 by a falling derrick. He died a hero since he was trying to save the team working under his supervision when he was killed.

Something unusual was discovered in March 1873. A coffin and its occupant were unearthed during the construction. No further mention was made of this discovery, and it remains a mystery. Why was the body not buried in a cemetery? The workers also found some cannonballs in the area of the eastern portal during the construction process. It was speculated that these cannonballs might have been fired during the American Revolution.

On April 18 around 5:00 p.m., Mr. Dudley, who was about eighteen years old, was seriously, and perhaps fatally, injured in Shaft no. 1 when a brick fell from the roof of the tunnel and struck him on the head. A physician removed part of his skull. The *Daily Dispatch* reported that it would be a "miracle if he recovered."

In late April, preparations had been made to blast away a large body of earth, and the order had been given for all the workmen to retire to a safe distance. But before the match was applied, the whole mass fell of its own weight. Xenophilus Frazier died instantly, and William Cozins was horribly crushed and was not expected to live. It was suspected that Frazier, being slightly deaf, might not have heard the order to get clear of the dynamite blast. Cozins was taken to his home, but a prominent Church Hill physician refused to treat him unless some responsible party would become surety for the payment. Quickly, another physician was summoned, and he provided prompt and kind attention.

On May 13, 1873, Britton Brown, an industrious, black brick mason, was severely cut and fell about fifteen feet to the bottom of the tunnel when a timber arch fell on him. It was believed that he would recover. The accidents continued.

The *Daily Dispatch* for May 22, 1873, reported that there was an accident at Shaft no. 2. Mr. C.M. Smith, assistant engineer, was taking observations when a slide occurred and partially covered him and a laborer who was assisting him. Both men escaped without serious injuries. The next day there was an accident at Shaft no.1. Earth had fallen into the tunnel; and while a man was inspecting it, another piece of earth fell and "struck him in the head, knocking him senseless and cutting his scalp very badly." The paper then noted that neither accident was a result of bad management or carelessness. In June, William Davis visited the tunnel where he had previously worked and went down Shaft no. 2 for the purpose of seeing some old friends. When trying to leave, he jumped on one of the cages bringing workers to the surface and was caught between the cage and the wall of the tunnel. Although his injuries appeared to be mortal, he was carried to the medical college where he, in the language of the times, rallied.

The tunnel was to be completed on October 1, 1873. The *Richmond Daily Dispatch* predicted: "Before the sun goes down the quiet shades of Chimborazo will re-echo the snort of the iron horse as it seeks to reach Tidewater before his long journey from the banks of the Ohio." This optimistic prediction

Construction scene at the west portal of the Church Hill Tunnel in 1872. Note the large number of African American workers. *Photograph courtesy of the Chesapeake and Ohio Historical Society.*

proved to be premature, for there was a small cave-in when the tunnel was just about completed. It appeared that in order to allow the passage of some material through the tunnel, some of the timbers supporting the tunnel had to be removed, thus weakening the tunnel. There was a great crash, leaving a hole in the ground about forty feet square and about thirty feet deep and taking with it a part of a shed. It took a long time to remove the debris from this cave-in. Surely this latest cave-in was frustrating, if not embarrassing, to all those who worked on the tunnel.

The almost mile-long tunnel was finally completed on November 25, 1873. The *Daily Dispatch* reported: "The last arching in the Church Hill Tunnel proper was finished yesterday morning." And then there was a tour of the tunnel for local dignitaries at the invitation of Mr. H.D. Whitcomb. The invited guests boarded a train and went as far as Shaft no. 3 where the recent cave-in had occurred. At this point, the party got out and watched the repairs being made on the tunnel and witnessed the laying of the last bricks in the tunnel arching. Upon squeezing through the "smallest aperture one could well imagine a man's body to be squeezed into while alive, the party came out on the other side within a short distance of the western portal, and in a few minutes the party got aboard the locomotive David Anderson Jr. [also reported as David Anderson]." This locomotive was somewhat of a celebrity since it had been used to pull the first train to go over the new tracks near Millers' Ferry. The party "had a pleasant run down to the company's wharves, below Rocketts on the James River." The invited guests believed the wharves were the best in Virginia, if not the nation. They also noted that the tracks through the tunnel were in very good order. Optimistically, it was observed that the cave-ins were now over because the arching was done and the tunnel was secure. Those on the train observed that "the tunnel is one of the longest and largest in the country, had been bored through the most treacherous earth, and its construction, as is well-known, was attended with many difficulties." It was further noted that the tunnel had been under construction for twenty-one months.

On November 29, 1873, there was another strike. Peter J. Rachleff noted that two hundred black laborers employed on the tunnel project went on strike. It was reported that their work was very dangerous. For these men, the pay was a maximum of one dollar per day, and because of a financial depression, several paydays had been missed. The laborers refused to work until they had been paid for work already performed. In response, the C&O replaced the black workers with two hundred newly arrived Italian immigrants. The black workers were never paid the money owed to them. Apparently, the Italians finished the tunnel.

And then it happened! The *Richmond Times-Dispatch* reported:

> *On Sunday, November 30, 1873, at about 11:00 a.m., C&O locomotive No. 2, the well-known David Anderson, Jr. which had been built in Richmond, pulled a car through the tunnel making it the first official trip through one of the largest tunnels in the county—a tunnel bored through the most treacherous earth and with the greatest difficulty.*

The opening of the tunnel attracted the attention of the national media. Numerous papers, including those in Columbia, South Carolina, and Washington, D.C., reported that "the Chesapeake and Ohio Railroad tunnel under Church Hill in Richmond, has been completed and trains will commence at once to run regularly through it."

Completion of the tunnel was a major engineering accomplishment. And the Richmond newspaper stated that "Mr. Whitcomb, chief engineer, and C.M. Bolton should be given all honors in recognition of their determination and skill in completing the tunnel which enabled C&O trains to pass through Richmond without any grade crossings."

Henry Drinker, in his analysis, wrote:

> *The Church Hill Tunnel may be said to have rivaled in difficulty of construction and in successful execution, under most trying obstacles, any tunnel-work ever attempted; and there are few engineers in the profession who can lay claim to have successfully passed through so trying an ordeal as Mr. Whitcomb, in his individual efforts in completing so long a line of difficult and heavy work, which had to be finished in a limited period of time...No man but a tunnel engineer can appreciate the difficulties and dangers of tunnel construction—it is not a question of calculating certain strains and allowing certain factors of safety, but a very vying with the unknown forces of darkness, all the more to be feared because one can never know what a day's advance may bring forth.*

In its annual reports, the Chesapeake and Ohio Railroad provided its stockholders updates on the progress of the Church Hill Tunnel. In October 1873, the railroad presented a lengthy report as to the problems associated with the tunnel. A portion of the report said:

> *The tunnel with its eastern approach* [because of the cave-ins] *has proved to be more troublesome and expensive than was anticipated. Every effort had been made to induce the contractors to hurry forward the masonry lining, but very little had been accomplished. With a view to aiding in this matter, a force of masons were employed on Company account on the 1st of November last year* [1872], *but with all the force we could get, the excavation preceded much faster then the arching* [which slowed up the construction process].

The report summarized the causes of the delays in the completion of the tunnel as accidents, increases in the costs of materials and landslides near the eastern portal. But the report ended on a very positive note: "This connection [by the Church Hill Tunnel] with tide-water passing through the City of Richmond, without any grade-crossings which will seriously

Chesapeake and Ohio officials at the tunnel during construction. Channing Bolton is standing at the extreme left. *Photograph courtesy of the Chesapeake and Ohio Historical Society.*

embarrass its operations, will prove to be invaluable to this Company, and perhaps to other companies, and will be worth all that it has cost."

In November 1873, the C&O again reported to its stockholders: "There are about seven miles of tunnels on the C&O...and all are completed, except the one under Church Hill in the City of Richmond, the actual cost of which has been much greater than the engineers estimated."

Although the tunnel had been built at great expense with bodies mangled and lives lost, its future use would determine if the cost in both lives and money was worthwhile. Only time would tell.

Chapter 5

Trains under Church Hill

With slamming roar...and thunderbolt light, the southbound train is gone in one projectile smash of wind-like fury, and the open empty silence of the passing fills us, thrills and stills us with the vision of Virginia in the moonlight, with the dream-still magic of Virginia in the moon.

—*Thomas Wolfe,* Of Time and the River

Now in operation, the tunnel's difficult construction had been completed. The dual tracks of the tunnel echoed with the sounds of clicking wheels, hissing air brakes, ringing bells and the occasional haunting sound of steam whistles to warn those who were using the tunnel as a shortcut to get off of the tracks. In addition to having a new tunnel, the C&O soon had a new name following a corporate reorganization. It was now to be known as the Chesapeake and Ohio Railway.

A C&O advertisement described a trip through Richmond via the tunnel:

> *From the James River wharves, the Chesapeake and Ohio Railway passes westerly across Bloody Run* [the site of a battle between Native Americans and the English located near the eastern portal] *and then through the Church Hill Tunnel into the Valley of the Shockoe Creek where are located the C&O's company offices, depot buildings, shops, and the distributing coal bins for the Richmond city trade.*

One passenger who rode the train through the tunnel was not impressed. The Reverend Paul Whitehead was a frequent passenger on trains that went through the tunnel. His comments about the tunnel reflected the tragic death of James Bolton who was killed while it was being constructed. He wrote: "James Bolton's life was sacrificed by the caving in of the Chesapeake and Ohio Tunnel under Church Hill—an ugly, dark hole that I never go through without a feeling of recoil, and which should have never been constructed." A female passenger felt the need to protect herself when passing through the dark tunnel. She was heard to say, "I carry a pistol in my pannier [basket]!"

With the tunnel and its location in Richmond, the C&O had the competitive advantage of offering the closest route from Richmond to the noted summer resorts in the Virginia Springs region where Richmonders and others would go to receive the real or perceived benefits of the warm natural springs. It was a yearly ritual for many people. In addition to going to the springs, the C&O passed though a beautiful region of the country marked by mountains, rivers, valleys and farmland.

Although Richmond had invested in the tunnel and the Chesapeake and Ohio trains were running through it, there were some complaints about the operation of the railroad. For example, Richmond's Committee on Police reported that "the C&O Railway would take such steps to abate the nuisance caused by the smoke from engines entering the Church Hill Tunnel from Seventeenth Street." There were a number of buildings and houses in the area at the time that apparently were being filled with smoke whenever a train came through the tunnel. The Phil G. Kelly whiskey warehouse was adjacent to the tracks at the western portal. The employees must have had a problem rolling whiskey barrels into the warehouse while inhaling smoke from steam locomotives passing through the tunnel on their way between the Seventeenth Street Yards and the Richmond docks.

There were a number of railroad accidents in the tunnel. In 1889, William Wade, a baggage agent, had a painful accident. He went down to the Church Hill Tunnel to meet an incoming train from Newport News; and in attempting to board the train, which was moving at a fair rate of speed, he slipped and fell across the track. People who witnessed the accident expected to see him cut to pieces by the car wheels, but with great presence of mind, he rolled off the track and escaped with a slight cut on the head and one on his foot. In 1894, the widow of Henry Coleman sued the C&O for $10,000 because of the death of her husband in the tunnel.

On at least one occasion, the tunnel achieved a measure of national attention. The *New York Times*, on April 20, 1892, directed its attention to the tunnel by reporting a potential problem. The boilers for the battleship USS *Texas* were built in Richmond at the Richmond Locomotive Works and needed to be shipped to Portsmouth, Virginia. But the boilers were too big to pass through the Church Hill Tunnel on a flatcar. The paper speculated that the boilers would be loaded at the shops on an immense carriage, rolled to the river, placed on a barge and thus transported to the navy yard. Somehow, the boilers must have arrived since the USS *Texas* fought in both world wars and is now a museum ship in Texas.

Although battleship boilers might not be able to pass through the tunnel because of their size, this was not a problem for the many excursion trains that would take Richmonders through the tunnel to the beaches for a weekend vacation. There was a report that a passenger on the Sacred Heart Excursion Train was thrown from the train as it was about to enter the tunnel. A police officer was summoned. Carrying a lantern, he searched the tunnel for the passenger. Upon completion of the search, it was concluded that the report must have been false since no one was found.

The C&O frequently advertised "Sunday Outings to Old Point, Newport News, Ocean View, and Norfolk for a $1.00 round trip." The advertisement further pointed out that "two fast trains with parlor cars over a stone ballast track, free of dust, and a sail across Hampton Roads, all combine to make the trip one to be enjoyed." These advertisements for various excursions on the railroad were run at a time when the railroads were the easiest way to reach summer vacation spots, including the Homestead at Hot Springs, Virginia, and the Greenbriar at White Sulphur Springs, West Virginia. I can recall going on the C&O to Buckroe Beach in the 1950s on church picnics. I even remember the conductor telling me that both the engineer and the fireman were over seventy-five years old. I still wonder if he was telling me the truth. For some reason, I do not think so.

Although excursion trains provided the opportunity for a good time for its passengers, the C&O also continued to profit from its docks on the James River at Richmond. These docks have long since disappeared, but they were state of the art when completed. They were double-deckers, meaning that ships could be loaded from the top dock at high tide and from the bottom dock at low tide. Initially, the docks were a profitable operation. Records show that by 1876, the C&O was carrying more than a quarter million tons of coal to Richmond for either local use or export. In a typical day in August 1881, the following ships were among those that arrived or departed from the Port of Richmond:

- steamer *Ariel* arrived from Norfolk with merchandise and passengers;
- schooner *Mary E. Morris* sailed from Richmond with pyrite; and
- schooner *Minnie Borgaen* sailed from Richmond with pine wood.

Unfortunately, Richmond's newfound importance as the terminal for an east–west mainline and a port city lasted for about eight years. Excellent docks and the Church Hill Tunnel could not make the James River deeper or straighter to accommodate the large oceangoing vessels being built at that time. The Richmond Common Council and the Richmond Chamber of Commerce had promised the C&O to deepen the James River to eighteen feet of water to accommodate coal ships. When blasting and dredging produced a channel less than fifteen feet deep, the C&O management felt released from its obligation to keep its eastern terminal in Richmond.

Since the shallow James River limited the potential of the Richmond docks, C.P. Huntington decided to extend the C&O tracks seventy-four more miles to Newport News, Virginia, and its extensive, natural deep-water harbor. Land was bought bordering Hampton Roads, and new port facilities were constructed with the approval of the Virginia General Assembly. The completion of this project in 1882 removed much of the traffic from the Church Hill Tunnel, which had been in use for less than ten years. Now trains rolled through Richmond to the new terminal without stopping. Richmond was no longer a primary destination for the C&O. A railroad executive summarized the situation when he reported that coal was dumped into ships on the James River at Fulton until 1882, when the Peninsula Division was opened to Newport News.

Even though Richmond was losing its status as a major port city, Richmonders seemed to have a deep affection for everyone associated with the C&O. The men and women of the Chesapeake and Ohio Railway were lauded by the *Richmond Times-Dispatch* when it reported that

> *strikes and trouble between the* [employees] *and the management are absolutely unknown. The patronage of the "drinking-saloon" has given place to the patronage of the Young Men's Christian Association buildings, the roughs have sought service among other lines, and all that class of accidents due to the carelessness or inefficiency of men have become as rare as derailments caused by bad track and defective cars.*

Although the C&O employees seemed to be exemplary employees and a credit to the railroad, if not the entire human race, arguments were made as to whether the investment in the tunnel was a good idea for Richmond.

Defenders of the use of government money for the tunnel argued that the problem was not with the C&O, but that it was

> *Richmond's great misfortune that the James River was not deepened 10 or 15 feet years ago. Had the James River been deepened as was promised, it may be doubted whether the Chesapeake and Ohio Railway Company would have considered it necessary to seek a port at the mouth of the river* [Newport News].

In addition, it was asserted that "without the tunnel the [C&O] might have switched off from the main[line] several miles above Richmond bypassing it completely." It was well known that a city without a railroad was destined for obscurity. In terms of investment, it was pointed out that the cost of the tunnel, tracks and wharves on the James River cost nearly $1 million, of which the city invested only about $300,000. It was also contended that the railroad never pledged itself not to seek a deep-water port.

Opponents against government funding of railroads used the tunnel as an example of a wasteful investment. It was pointed out that Richmond had gone wild over the Church Hill Tunnel and spent $300,000 on the tunnel and then repented when the tunnel was relegated to limited use and eventual obscurity, with its portals becoming a trellis for vines. Government leaders also reminded people that they had invested money to prevent Richmond from being a way station on the Chesapeake and Ohio Railroad, but Richmonders could now sit on the hillside and watch the trains run by to Newport News. The Church Hill Tunnel helped put the trains into Richmond; but Richmond could not keep them because it did not have a deep-water port that could compete with the deep-water ports in Tidewater.

By 1901, the tunnel was rarely used, but there were still accidents in the tunnel. In June 1901, Engine no. 237 was pulling a long train of cars. The train had entered the western portal of the tunnel when the last sixteen cars became uncoupled without the knowledge of the engineer and were left standing unattended on the tracks. In the meantime, Engine no. 319, pulling a caboose, left the Seventeenth Street Yards and entered the dark tunnel. Because of the darkness of the tunnel, the engineer did not see the sixteen cars that had been left unattended in the tunnel and crashed into them. The engineer and the conductor were slightly injured, and a number of the cars were knocked off of the track. The tunnel remained blocked until a work train came and removed the damaged cars and replaced the track.

In 1902, the last scheduled train passed through the tunnel. It was now little more than a sidetrack. The days of trains passing under Church Hill were about to end, but the tunnel continued to assert itself.

Around the time it was relegated to limited use, there was an unsettling headline in the *Richmond Times* on March 12, 1902. The headline read: "Depression over Church Hill Tunnel." It was reported that recent rain had weakened the tunnel and it was in danger of caving in. The paper further

Postcard showing the east portal when the tunnel was in operation. *Special Collection and Archives, Virginia Commonwealth University Library.*

reported that there was already a slight depression that could collapse and destroy about thirty houses in the East End of Richmond. People felt that a thunderstorm or earthquake would cause a disaster; however, the tunnel did not cave in, and city officials tended to downplay the situation. Once again, the water-soaked soil of Church Hill began to settle.

Ironically, water had played a significant role in the history of the Church Hill Tunnel. A prehistoric ocean made the construction of the tunnel difficult; the James River made the Church Hill Tunnel necessary; and a modern-day deep-water port at Newport News helped to put the tunnel out of business. But the Church Hill Tunnel would not be forgotten—it would reassert itself in the future. It was only a matter of time.

Chapter 6

A Viaduct, a Station and a Three-Level Crossing

The station, as he entered it, was murmurous with the immense and distant sound of time.
—*Thomas Wolfe*, You Can't Go Home Again

Bottom's Up Pizza, a restaurant that my family and I enjoy, is located almost under the C&O Viaduct. Amid the talking and laughing of the pizza eaters, there is the frequent "rumble and roar" of CSX locomotives, as they pull long trains on a viaduct almost over the restaurant. I am sure that most of the customers do not know that several boxcars once fell off the viaduct and crashed to the streets below.

The story of the viaduct and a new station were featured in the *Richmond Dispatch* of December 20, 1885. The proposed viaduct, if built, would render the Church Hill Tunnel virtually obsolete. Whereas the tunnel was an underground solution to a problem, the viaduct would be an aboveground solution to another problem. The C&O had great difficulty in transferring cars from its James River Division to its Peninsula Division. Harry Frazier, chief engineer of the C&O, described the problem in this way: "There was a fly in the ointment for smooth freight train movement through Richmond between the James River and the Peninsula Divisions."

Frazier further explained:

> *All James River Division freight trains stopped at the old Richmond and Alleghany Yards and roundhouse, at the foot of Second Street, where they were reduced in length and moved by other power on a single-track wooden trestle, high on its upper end that descended on a steep grade from Twelfth Street to the main track on the York River Division of the Richmond and Danville, and over the rails of that company to another single-track wooden trestle owned by the C&O, which ascended on a similar steep grade to Fulton Yard.*

This certainly seemed to be a complicated way to transfer trains from one place to another, and it was not conducive to the smooth operation of a railroad.

There were two proposals made by engineers to eliminate this bottleneck. One plan provided for a line from the James River Division above Richmond that crossed over to and down Bacon Quarter Branch (a small stream that at one time flowed from the area of the Boulevard meandering eastward into Shockoe Creek) to a connection with C&O tracks that passed through the Church Hill Tunnel to reach Fulton. The second proposal was to build a very high viaduct from the canal basin at Twelfth Street, to and via Dock Street and across the Gas Works property to Fulton. Both of these plans were rejected by C&O officials.

The first proposal was rejected because of the heavy adverse grades in both directions that made it equivalent to another operating division; the second was rejected because the proposed viaduct was too high in some places. But Chief Engineer Frazier felt that the best solution was the viaduct, which would, in effect, push the whole end of the railroad line into the James River. Frazier then worked out a plan where the viaduct would connect the James River and Peninsula Divisions with a double-track viaduct.

Frazier's plan was unique. Although bridges usually cross streams and rivers, his proposal was that a nearly mile-long bridge, to be known as a viaduct, would be in the river and then return to land on the same side of the river where it entered. Frazier summed up the viaduct proposal by writing: "The design was regarded as a bold stroke by the technical papers of the time. The whole length of the structure is about three miles."

When construction got underway in the late 1890s, the building of the viaduct, like the construction of the tunnel, was seen as one of the greatest improvements in railroad transportation that Richmond had ever seen, and its construction was frequently reported on in the daily papers. The *Richmond Times* reported, "The building of the Chesapeake and Ohio Viaduct is an interesting sight, as there is something attractive in seeing iron sills of giant proportions lifted and lowered into place with as much apparent ease as if they were trifles as light as air." The paper also noted

> *that the crane being used in the construction was the largest in the United States and the second largest in the world. Huge pieces of iron weighing many tons were lifted into place like mere straws. They were bolted into place, the track laid, then the crane was moved onto the completed part and another span began.*

It was also reported that "there were dynamite blasts which sent the workers scurrying for shelter while the spectators flinched, jumped, and were startled as much as a gun-shy dog." In addition, passengers on southbound trains from Richmond were impressed with the rapid progress being made in the construction of the viaduct. Even though the viaduct was being built rapidly, the foreman did not permit his men to work in bad weather since he did not think it would accomplish very much; however, he did augment his workforce with bridge workers from Pennsylvania and North Carolina. In a progress report, the *Richmond Dispatch* noted: "The viaduct is coming down the [James] river steadily [from the area of Hollywood Cemetery], while from Fulton the work is being rapidly pushed." The plan was for the two crews to meet and join the viaduct together. Hopefully, the additional workers would speed up the process.

By June 1901, the viaduct was nearing completion when it was reported that two cranes were used to put four large girders in place to span Seventeenth and Cary Streets. But like the tunnel, there were problems with the construction of the viaduct. To avoid electric shock from the nearby trolley lines, boards were put under the steel girders to insulate them in case they came into contact with the electric line. The *Richmond Dispatch* reported a very unusual accident:

> *By a remarkable combination of circumstances, one of the boards had a nail in it, and that nail touched the live wire with one end and the steel girder with the other. Frank Farmer was at one end of the board and about 15 feet from the girder. The nail completed the circuit, and Farmer, as a result, fell off his perch as if he had been shot. His foot caught in the iron lace-work which held the double girder together, and by this means he was held suspended until workers rushed to his aid and relieved him of the embarrassing situation. When he was taken down, he was slightly stunned but was soon himself again.*

And then, railroad history was made in Richmond. On June 24, 1901, at two fifty in the morning, the first train passed over the newly completed viaduct. The train consisted of a yard engine and several coal cars and was run from the Second Street Yards to Fulton. The engine was no. 299, the engineer was Jos. Ladd, Gordon was the fireman and McGruder was the conductor. The viaduct was not only unique for going beside, instead of crossing, the river, but it also completed a three-level crossing in the area just south of Main Street Station at Byrd Street.

On the ground level were the Southern Railway tracks that were in place during the Civil War. For many years, the Southern Railway carried passengers from Richmond to West Point, Virginia. Passing above the Southern tracks was a second viaduct that was the mainline of the Seaboard Airline Railroad. This viaduct, in fact, was both an overpass and an underpass since it was sandwiched between the two other railroad lines. The Seaboard Railroad was built to take advantage of the Florida traffic and was known for running through the "Heart of Dixie." It had trains with names such as the Robert E. Lee, the Southern States Special and the Orange Blossom Special. These trains provided "air-conditioned meals that appeased air-conditioned appetites." Above the Seaboard Viaduct was the new Chesapeake and Ohio Viaduct, which carried the mainline of the James River Division. When built it was, and probably still is, the only triple-railroad crossing in the world. Postcards were sold with the caption "Is two over one fare [*sic*]"? These postcards were updated over the years, and each showed more modern equipment. The new viaduct further diminished the use of the tunnel that Richmonders had invested in, and that had been a challenge to build. A second phase in the building plan was a new station for the Chesapeake and Ohio.

Richmonders learned about the proposed Main Street Station in 1899 when the *Richmond Times* published the plans for a new station to serve the Chesapeake and Ohio and Seaboard Airline Railroads. The station was to be built on the north side of Main Street between Fifteenth and Seventeenth Streets. The new depot was to be "one of the greatest improvements in Richmond in recent years." Indeed, it was described as "modern in every appointment…one of the most attractive stations in the country. Of 'French Renaissance' style, it was to be a magnificent gateway to the City of Richmond."

Because of the frequent flooding of the nearby James River, the first floor of the station was built above flood level. Upon entering the first floor and buying a ticket, passengers could walk up the stairs or ride the elevator to the second floor where they could board the trains. Trains entered and departed the station under a massive train shed that was built behind the station. The third and fourth floors of the station were used for office space. To some, the station appeared to be a great chateau built in downtown Richmond.

Upon completion, the new Main Street Station was an instant Richmond landmark, but its opening was without fanfare. On November 27, 1901, the *Richmond Times* reported that "at 12:40 p.m., train No.1 of the Chesapeake and Ohio Railway steamed into the station from Newport News, Virginia. The train was eight minutes late according to the clock in the station's tower." Even though there was no formal opening of the station, thousands of people were on hand to welcome the train. It was reported that with so many spectators at the station, the passengers had difficulty getting out of the passenger cars.

Those at the station commented that "the insistent cries of the hotel porters, the long lines of hacks, carriages, and busses gave one a clear idea they were in a railway station, if there had been any doubt." Many of the spectators had left when the first Seaboard Airline train arrived at the station from points south. Those who remained welcomed Seaboard train no. 38 that was carrying the first bridal couple to arrive at the station. The new station was now open for business.

A newspaper reporter who was on the first C&O train to leave the station wrote:

> *The shades of evening were falling as the train backed out of the train shed. Up and down Main Street could be seen numerous streetcars and the busy*

Postcard showing the three-level crossing created by the completion of the C&O Viaduct. *Special Collection and Archive, Virginia Commonwealth University Library.*

> *turmoil of the city's population hurrying through with the day's work…The engine's headlight* [was] *burning a way into the darkness that stretched to the westward where the sun had hidden behind the everlasting hills.*

In the summer of 1933, my parents eloped on a train from Main Street Station. My mother frequently told me that a conductor who knew them saw them board the train. Although he spotted them, he promised not to tell anyone. After arriving home, he did tell his wife that there was going to be a wedding, but that was all he ever said. Their secret was safe as they rode to the nation's capital to get married.

Whenever I look at that station, I remember my mother's stories about the day my parents took my uncle to the station to leave to fight in World War II, of the many church trips I took to the beaches of Virginia and the excitement of seeing powerful locomotives entering and leaving the station. Does anyone ever get over the excitement of seeing a locomotive coming down the tracks? I have not!

Chapter 7

The Extension and Closing of the Church Hill Tunnel

The night is born, and the stars awake
While the moon ascends the sky;
A ghostly wind stirs a lonely lake
To the wail of a loon's weird cry,
And the vines creep up to the broken door
Of a station where man will come no more.
—Olin Lyman, "Abandoned"

The Church Hill Tunnel was not in regular use, but there were occasional news stories about it. In 1904, a train crew was working near the tunnel when a train hit a streetcar that was crossing the tracks. Although the streetcar was turned into kindling, there were no serious injuries reported.

The tunnel briefly was returned to service in 1912 when an earth slide blocked the approach to the gashouse in Fulton, and coal and other supplies for the plant were routed through the tunnel for about thirty days. The tunnel was seeing only limited use, but there was a plan to extend the eastern end of the tunnel but not for the benefit of the C&O.

The initial plans for the extension of the tunnel can be traced back to around 1902 when an article in the *Richmond Dispatch* proposed the extension of Grace Street. The article stated, "In order for the city to fill the deep ravine between Twenty-ninth Street and Chimborazo Hill, it is necessary for the Chesapeake and Ohio Company to construct an arch over its road from the eastern end of the Church Hill Tunnel as far east as the fill will extend." Of course, there was no way the city could force the C&O to take such action since the tunnel was no longer essential to their operation.

It was almost ten years before formal action was finally taken on this proposal. On December 13, 1912, the City of Richmond authorized the extension of the tunnel. The enabling ordinance said:

> *Be it resolved by the Council of the City of Richmond, the Board of Alderman concurring: That the Mayor of the City of Richmond be, and is hereby authorized and directed, on behalf of the City of Richmond... to enter into a written contract with the Chesapeake and Ohio Railway Company, a corporation, providing for the extension of the eastern end of the Church Hill Tunnel one hundred and twenty-five (125) feet eastwardly from its present eastern portal.*

In 1913, at the cost of $20,000, a 24-foot extension was added to the eastern end of the tunnel so that a section of Grace Street could be filled in.

Locomotive 231 while in the service of the Chicago, Cincinnati and Louisville Railroad.
Photograph courtesy of the Railway and Locomotive Historical Society.

This extension made the final length of the tunnel 4,168 feet. Although the extension was complete, the tunnel was soon rendered impassable. In 1915, some weakened timbers were found in the tunnel, and they were reinforced with other timbers; thus, the tunnel was blocked and put out of service. The tunnel, whose construction had cost a number of lives and a great deal of money, was no longer in use except as a shortcut for school children and others willing to brave the dark, eerie hole under the ground by using a paper torch as their only source of light.

Chapter 8

The Tunnel Is Returned to Use

The Rails go westward in the dark. Brother, have you seen starlight on the rails? Have you heard the thunder of the fast express?
—*Thomas Wolfe,* Of Time and the River

The C&O decided to repair and reopen the Church Hill Tunnel after it had been abandoned for about ten years. This decision was made because of the overcrowded conditions on the viaduct, which were a result of the increased volume of traffic that had come to the C&O. In its present condition, the Church Hill Tunnel could not relieve this influx of traffic because it was blocked with timbers, and it could not accommodate the larger locomotives and cars that were being acquired by the C&O. But if the tunnel was repaired, enlarged and strengthened, it could accommodate the larger locomotives and freight cars, which would remove some of the traffic that was causing bottlenecks on the overcrowded viaduct. Freight trains could use the reopened tunnel and bypass the crowded Main Street Station on their way to and from the Seventeenth Street and Fulton Yards. Since the tunnel was already built, it seemed a logical decision to refurbish and return it to service.

In some of the contemporary media, there were statements that suggest that the tunnel was simply being braced, not restored for use, to relieve the anxiety of the Church Hill landowners who were afraid of another cave-in; however, the preponderance of the evidence suggested that the tunnel was being repaired to return it to use.

The officials of the C&O believed this work could best be accomplished by inserting large concrete rings into the old tunnel that would both enlarge and render it secure, removing the constant threat of cave-ins and related problems that had plagued the tunnel since it was first constructed. To accomplish this enlargement process, many workers were employed by the railroad to do the work. Like the men who had dug the tunnel in the 1870s, they were about to learn that the Church Hill Tunnel was a dangerous place to work. And it should be remembered that the same soil, which had caused so many of the problems when the tunnel had been dug, was still there, holding the potential for causing a cave-in in a tunnel that was now called by many the "Tunnel of Death."

Chapter 9

Friday, October 2, 1925

Remember the Church Hill Tunnel,
Near a mile under Richmond Town
There's a story I want to tell you
Of a train that'll never be found
—Llewellyn Lewis, "The Train That Will Never Be Found"

It was cool and rainy on Friday, October 2, 1925, but the laborers working inside the tunnel, removing earth, lifting beams and mixing concrete, stayed dry. These laborers, directed by their supervisors, were digging into the walls and under the foundation of the tunnel in order to enlarge it so the large concrete rings could be slipped into place. There were also skilled tunnel men fitting the supports into place and placing the arches in preparation for the placement of the concrete rings; there were carpenters cutting timbers and fitting concrete forms; and there were locomotives pulling work trains into the tunnel to be filled with dirt and debris by laborers and then hauled out again. Around two hundred men would be working in the tunnel until the work was completed.

Much of the initial work of the enlargement was being carried on just inside the western portal of the tunnel near the Marshall Street Viaduct and next to the T.W. Wood and Sons seed warehouse. This was the same area where ground was first broken for the tunnel in 1871. In fact, these laborers were performing many of the same tasks of digging and hauling that other laborers had performed over fifty years ago.

While the men were working, Thomas Joseph Mason, a C&O engineer with forty-four years of service, kissed his wife goodbye, left his house and headed to the Fulton Yard. His daughter was going to have a tonsillectomy that day, and he promised to give her five dollars and a doll with long hair when he returned. Tom Mason was almost at the corner of the block when he turned around, went back to see his wife and kissed her again. Did he have a premonition that something was going to happen? Finally, Tom Mason went to work on the railroad as he had done since he was a teenager.

Shortly before 3:00 p.m. that day, in the Fulton Yard of the Chesapeake and Ohio Railway, Tom Mason climbed into the cab of C&O locomotive no. 231. Next to him in the cab was his fireman, Benjamin Franklin Mosby. Locomotive no. 231 was classified as an American Class locomotive. It had four leading wheels, four driving wheels, but no trailing wheels under the cab. These locomotives were lightweight and had excellent riding stability, which was needed to travel the rough tracks of the early railroads that were being built at a rapid pace to meet the needs of a growing industrialized nation.

Although Tom Mason probably did not know it, the locomotive assigned to him was originally built for the Chicago, Cincinnati and Louisville Railroad by the Baldwin Locomotive Works in 1903, and its engine number on that railroad was 54. When the C&O acquired the bankrupt Chicago, Cincinnati and Louisville Railroad, it obtained locomotive no. 54. Throughout its service on two railroads, the locomotive had several different road numbers, but on this day, no. 231 was painted in large numbers on its tender. It is known that this locomotive had been used on a run to Orange, Virginia, pulling a passenger train while in the service of the C&O. With a headlight mounted atop the boiler, a tall smokestack and a bell, it was typical of the locomotives of its generation; however, since it was old, it was now being used as a switch engine pulling a work train.

Tom Mason and Ben Mosby, who was called at the last minute to substitute for an ill fireman, were ready to pull ten flatcars into the tunnel so that the laborers could load them with the dirt and other material being removed during the construction process. Other members of the train crew were G.C. McFadden, conductor, and C.S. Kelso and A.G. Adams, brakemen.

Methodically, while looking at the dials and the gauges in front of him, the engineer performed the ritual of releasing the air brakes and slowly

Locomotive 231, which was trapped in the Church Hill Tunnel. This picture shows it in passenger service at Orange, Virginia. *Photograph courtesy of the Chesapeake and Ohio Historical Society.*

opening the throttle. The fireman shoveled coal into the firebox as the train slowly got underway. The hissing steam could be heard, and the smoke from the locomotive could be seen in the air over Fulton Yard as the train headed for the tunnel. With the locomotive's driving wheels turning and its pistons hissing, the work train pulled out of Fulton Yard destined for destruction. Tom Mason crossed the bridge over Williamsburg Road and then saw the light of day for the last time when he pulled through a ravine and entered the eastern portal of the tunnel. In the dark tunnel, the headlight of locomotive 231 painted the sides of the tunnel like some magical paintbrush. The underground train crossed under Broad Street near St. Patrick's Catholic Church where Tom Mason and his family worshipped and almost under St. John's Episcopal Church where Fireman Mosby and his family attended church.

After a run for about a mile through the tunnel, the train was approximately fifty to one hundred feet from the western portal underneath Twentieth Street. Reaching the work area, Tom Mason applied the air brakes to stop the train. The hissing air brakes echoed in the tunnel along with the sound of metal hitting metal as the train came to a stop. With the train stopped, the engineer told the brakeman to uncouple the string of flatcars so the laborers could start filling them with dirt and debris. With the cars uncoupled, Tom Mason once again released the air brakes and opened the throttle. The pistons hissed steam, and the drivers turned as the locomotive slowly headed toward the daylight of the western portal on what was supposed to be Tom Mason's last day on this particular run. The next day, he was to report to the C&O for a new assignment.

As the train was slowly steaming and hissing toward the western portal, a few bricks from the tunnel's roof fell with a splash into pools of water on the tunnel floor. The falling bricks caused the electrical connections in the tunnel to break and the work lights to flicker twice before they went out, plunging the entire tunnel into total darkness.

The sudden darkness, along with the ominous sounds of falling bricks splashing in the puddles on the tunnel's floor, alarmed the workers. Something had obviously gone wrong. The workers did not know what was happening, but they were terrified. Surely, they were aware of the tunnel's history of cave-ins and the caution the work crews had been told to use while working in the tunnel. Was this the start of another collapse or just a loose brick falling from the ceiling? The *Richmond Times-Dispatch* reported that "the laborers started to run to the tunnel's eastern portal in the darkness because they knew something was wrong and they were not going to wait around to see what might happen." The paper noted, "When the laborers escaped from the tunnel, they refused medical attention even though they were injured. Instead, they scattered to all sections of Richmond following their miraculous escape from the chamber of death." A routine day had just become a day that was anything but routine—it was a day marked for disaster.

Hearing the cracking of the bricks and seeing the earth coming down upon them, B.F. Mosby, the fireman on the locomotive, yelled, "Watch out Tom [Mason] she's a-coming in." Seconds later, approximately 150 feet of the tunnel's roof fell, burying locomotive 231 and its crew. The two men in the locomotive cab heard the awful sounds of the tunnel caving in and watched in horror as it crushed the locomotive. With its boiler crushed, steam sprayed all over both Mosby and Mason. Mason could not escape. He was trapped in the locomotive. He could only sit and endure the horrible, excruciating pain from the shower of boiling water pouring over his body. Scalded by the escaping water from the crushed locomotive, Mosby had severe burns from his waist up from the boiling water that even penetrated his heavy work clothing. He also suffered a cut over his right eye. Although in unbearable pain from the burns, Mosby was able to slip out of the locomotive's cab, get on the ground and crawl under the flatcars behind the train that kept the falling dirt off him and served as an escape route within a collapsing tunnel. Like a mole, he managed to crawl out and headed toward the eastern portal.

Unlike his fireman, Engineer Mason was a large man and could not slide out of the locomotive's cab and seek safety. He remained at the throttle, burning in agony. Tom Mason was to meet his fate in a crumbling tunnel. His coffin would have 231 painted on its side.

As Fireman Mosby struggled toward the eastern portal, a number of men tried to help him, but they were unaware of how badly he was burned and how painful their touch must have been to him. Every step the fireman took must have been sheer torture, but he continued to stumble toward the daylight at the eastern end of the tunnel. Other railroaders continued to try to help the fireman as he continued his odyssey of escape that would lead him to safety over three-quarters of a mile away. When he emerged from the collapsing tunnel and stumbled into the cold rain that was falling outside, he asked for some water and said, "Some of you boys please call my wife and tell her I got out and I am not badly hurt." The scalded man, whose upper body had most of the skin burned off, was wracked with pain, but he had the caring and loving spirit to want his wife, Marie, and little girl, Dorothy Marie, to know he was alive.

Mosby escaped through the eastern portal less than an hour after the cave-in. Because of the scalds and boiled skin, he insisted on struggling up the steep, dirt bank beside the tunnel without help since he was in too much pain to be carried on a stretcher or even touched. Gingerly, he got into a *News Leader* reporter's taxicab and was rushed to Grace Hospital, which was several miles away. The brave fireman, who never screamed in pain, who managed to struggle almost a mile to get out of the tunnel, whose first thoughts were of his family and who said he was not badly hurt, died seven hours later. He left his wife a widow and his daughter without a father. The tunnel had claimed another life. There would be more.

Although Mosby escaped, no one was giving up on trying to save the engineer or any other man who might be trapped. R.C. Gary, foreman of the train crew that was at work near the eastern end of the tunnel, braved death when he ran the length of the tunnel to see if he could assist those who were trapped, including Tom Mason. He got to the stricken locomotive and made a desperate effort to get Mason out, but the engineer was pinned by debris and the reverse lever, which was lodged firmly across his chest. Even a determined and desperate man like Gary could not accomplish the impossible.

Against almost incredible odds, other men continued the heroic effort to save Mason and anyone else that they could find by entering the eastern portal and running toward the cave-in. Dr. Aaron Seldes, a Fulton physician, braved death and injury when he went into the tunnel and fought his way to the string of flatcars near the imprisoned engineer. He unfortunately had to turn back when he found additional progress was impossible because of the impenetrable debris. Equally courageous was a *Richmond Times-Dispatch* reporter who did more than report news. Like Dr. Seldes, he tried to reach the trapped engineer by going through the eastern portal, but he was unable to get around, across or under the solid mass of earth that would have taken a steam shovel to move. It could not be moved by the scratching, pawing and pounding of desperate human hands.

Desperate men were trying to save desperate men, but it proved impossible. Before long, foul air forced an almost complete abandonment of the initial work by the rescue crews working in the tunnel's eastern portal. But people still waited outside of the eastern portal in the forlorn hope that other men might miraculously emerge from the dark tunnel and into the light of day.

Arriving at the tunnel was Mrs. Mary Mason, Tom Mason's wife. She had only been home for a few minutes after having left her daughter at St. Luke's Hospital following the girl's tonsillectomy when there was a knock at the door. Her son-in-law arrived with the terrible news of the cave-in. Mrs. Mason immediately went to the tunnel in the fervent hope that her husband would be found alive. Surely, she remembered the second kiss he gave her when he returned to his house for no apparent reason. Did Tom Mason have a premonition of death? Was this the reason for the second kiss?

The engine crew in the locomotive was not the only one that tried to escape death from the foul hole in the ground. According to the *Richmond Times-Dispatch*, "Three gangs of laborers under Division Engineer S.H. Pulliam were at work repairing the ancient tunnel to return it to use at the time of the accident." Two of the work gangs were laborers; the third one was a carpenter gang. The tunnel workers who were to load the flatcars

Tom Mason had pulled through the tunnel were about to face death in a collapsing tunnel.

A.G. Adams, the flagman on the doomed train, was standing on a flatcar next to the locomotive when a few bricks began to fall and splash in the water on the tunnel floor. On the flatcar with him were R.W. Poindexter, labor foreman, and train crewmen C.S. Kelso and G.C. McFadden. The falling bricks from the roof of the tunnel knocked all of the men down. Thinking quickly, they crawled beneath the flatcars, which protected them from the collapsing tunnel, as it had provided an escape route for Ben Mosby.

Adams recalled the collapse in some detail:

> *I was standing up on the car when the first bricks started to fall. Something knocked me from the flatcar into the side ditch of the tunnel. A moment later, I dove underneath the car almost before I realized that the tunnel was coming in on us…There were other men under the flatcars in the darkness. We heard a great scrambling of men. I did not know what they were talking about and those of us who were hurt did not know we had been injured…We were there* [under the flatcars] *for many minutes, 10 or 15 I suppose, while the noise of the slide continued. Then every man pushed out the best way he could.*

Adams, along with Kelso and McFadden, was helped to find his way out of the tunnel by a man with a lantern that provided him the much needed light to pierce through the eerie darkness. The men who were saved by the flatcars now headed toward the eastern portal and safety. A reporter wrote: "The train crew one by one, struggled like ants to the eastern end of the tunnel." They had no way of knowing whether more of the tunnel would collapse on them. It took the group about thirty minutes before they reached safety and escaped being buried under tons of dirt. Once outside, Adams, who was telling his story while sitting in a supply shack, suddenly realized for the first time that he had been injured. He exclaimed, "Doggone if my side doesn't hurt. A rock or something must have hit me. I hadn't realized it before."

These three men received medical attention shortly after the critically burned Mosby. McFadden was treated for a broken arm; the other men had minor injuries. While at the hospital, Adams learned that Tom Mason was still trapped in his locomotive. Leaving his two friends at the hospital,

Postcard showing Jefferson Park around 1910. *Special Collection and Archives, Virginia Commonwealth University Library.*

he returned to the scene of the cave-in in spite of his injuries. He wanted to help in the rescue effort.

Because the cave-in blocked the western portal, most of the men who escaped ran to the eastern portal, but there were some exceptions. Lemy Campbell, a laborer, was one of the few workers who escaped being crushed to death by running out of the western portal. He was working near the tunnel's western portal when disaster struck. Like the other workers, he heard the bricks fall, as well as a cracking sound that warned of danger. Realizing what was lurking, he made a break for the still open western portal. As he was running, the roof of the tunnel crashed in behind him. He narrowly escaped being crushed to death by the falling tunnel. Other workers who reportedly escaped though the western portal were R.J. Salmons and Willie White. The *Richmond News Leader* reported: "All of these men were knocked down by the tidal wave of compressed air forced through the [tunnel] by the collapse."

Once out of the tunnel, Lemy Campbell huddled beneath a wooden beam that afforded him some protection from the rain and the opportunity to think about his close brush with death. He watched the rescue crews haul braces into the tunnel in an effort to stop any more cave-ins.

Carpenters working near the western portal under the supervision of R.W. Poindexter had just been "cut loose" when they felt a sharp swish of air, like the swish felt by those who were building the tunnel when it caved in while it was under construction in the early 1870s. The panicked workers immediately abandoned their work, dropped their tools and ran a long, dark mile through the tunnel until they escaped through the eastern portal. Escaping from the dark hole they saw the welcome relief of the rain that was falling outside.

While many men had escaped from the tunnel, a major concern was whether there were other men still trapped in the tunnel along with Tom Mason. Initial estimates of those missing ranged from forty to one hundred men; however, a more accurate count was needed. Upon checking the company roster, it was determined that only Tom Mason and two laborers, Richard Lewis and H. Smith, were still missing. The two missing laborers were supervised by R.W. Poindexter, who initially reported four of the laborers were missing. But the other two, G. Brown and H. Barnes, eventually turned up as having escaped and left the area. Were Lewis and Smith trapped in the tunnel under tons of dirt, or had they escaped and left the area with a profound sense of relief? Poindexter did not leave the tunnel for over an hour. He delayed his escape and put his life at risk to see if he could help others who might have been trapped. A small man, Poindexter finally wormed his way out through the piles of dirt and debris. It was believed that he was the supervisor of most of the men missing in the tunnel. When he left the tunnel, he realized that he had come within a "scratch" of being caught in the deathtrap; and after making his way out of the pile of mud, he remained on the outside to see if he could help.

The C&O officials concluded that only two men were missing and the engineer was trapped, but not everyone agreed that the count was accurate. Experienced railroad men felt that many more men were trapped in the cave-in. They claimed that a new construction gang had been taken on that morning, but that they had not had their names added to the company roster. Other men pointed out that some men had entered the tunnel to seek employment just before the cave-in and were not on the official roster. This is certainly a possibility because black laborers would frequently seek work on the railroad. Other railroaders believed that anywhere from ten to fifteen men were still trapped under the sliding debris that closed the tunnel. But this could not be ascertained until rescuers entered the tunnel, found the crushed locomotive and removed the dirt that had buried any remaining workers in the tomb called the Church Hill Tunnel.

Just as there were accounts of those who escaped, there were also stories of the general panic that gripped the men when the earth fell on them. Adams reported, "We heard men calling and screaming through the darkness." George T. Raborg, a carpenter foreman, who was working about fifty feet from the cave-in, reported the panic that gripped the men who were trying to escape with their lives.

He recalled,

> *A moment after the noise of the first bricks falling came the crash; the lights went out; Hell began to reign in the tunnel. Men passed me screaming and fighting. Some of them yelled that they had knives and would cut anybody that got in their way. Others were praying—you never heard such praying. The confusion lasted for a long time, it seemed. There were no lights. No one thought to even light a match. Men ran back and forth bewildered. They lost direction in the darkness and did not know where to run. Some of them ran toward where the dirt was falling until warned by the noise. They then quickly headed the other way. Other men butted their heads into the sidewalls, fell over the ties and rails, and knocked each other down in their desperate effort to escape death. And to make matters worse, a wave of compressed air from the falling tunnel blew a dozen men off of their feet.*
>
> *The tunnel resounded with the roar of falling clay and with the screams of maddened men rushing through the blackness to safety or to death—they did not know which one would claim them. It was a grand mess, and everyone was scared with good reason. They had just escaped death under a pile of dirt.*

Panic-struck men commented "that being in the tunnel was like being in a bottomless pit without knowing what had happened or what was going to happen." Comments from other observers were in the same vein. To avoid death, men were fighting through the darkness, crying, shrieking and stumbling blindly. Under Jefferson Park and the city's streets, they ran, guided by hands that felt along the tunnel walls in order to find a way to the outside world and a renewed chance to live.

When all the accounts of escape were compared, most of the men told essentially the same story: they heard the bricks fall prior to the cave-in, they recalled the splash of the bricks into the water and then the massive cave-in. Everyone felt the rush of air, which was strong enough to knock men off their feet. Regardless of the accounts, there was no question that there had been a disaster of unknown magnitude at the tunnel, and the news of the disaster began to spread from the area of the cave-in to the city and beyond.

Even though there were few radios, news of the disaster traveled quickly through the Richmond community, giving rise to both rumors and truth. In Barton Heights, in Richmond's Northside, it was believed that a streetcar filled with passengers had plunged off the Marshall Street Viaduct. People knew that streetcars ran across the viaduct, and a disaster of this nature seemed plausible. And then another story began to circulate that the entire Marshall Street Viaduct had collapsed, carrying both cars and streetcars to their doom. Other sections of Richmond heard that all of Church Hill had slid into Shockoe Valley. As the location of the disaster became known, the rumors began to have some degree of truth. For example, reports began to indicate that a passenger train with five coaches had been caught in a cave-in and had blown up, killing most of the passengers. Another rumor claimed that several hundred workers had perished in the tunnel. Eventually, the truth began to emerge about the cave-in of the Church Hill Tunnel.

Richmond was a city of railroads and railroad men. The citizens of Richmond were accustomed to seeing the giant Chesapeake and Ohio locomotives race down the tracks through the city. Many of these same people, as well as the children who waved at the engineers as their trains sped down the tracks, probably knew or knew of a railroad man who might be trapped in the tunnel.

As the truth and the location of the cave-in became known, people gathered at the site of the disaster. They seemed to be drawn to the area by a mysterious force that seemed to attract onlookers to all disasters, including the Church Hill Tunnel. The curious and the concerned were as one, as they arrived to gape at what was the side of Jefferson Park. They could not see the chaos in the tunnel, but they could see the cracks and broken steps on the side of Jefferson Park.

As more people heard of the disaster, large crowds began to gather at the park. Before long, thousands of residents of Church Hill and the city gathered and looked at the yawning chasm where the hillside had slipped and crumpled into the C&O tunnel between Nineteenth and Twentieth Streets.

Among the first to arrive on the scene was a young boy who had just learned that his father had been caught in the tunnel. Ralph Mason would maintain a vigil at the tunnel for the next nine days and would fervently hope that his father would be found alive. (There are authorities who believed that the newspaper was in error and that it was not Mason's son who was at the tunnel but another family member.)

A nearby resident, Helen Williams, stood in the once beautiful Jefferson Park, with its well-manicured tennis court, fountain and park house, and looked at the wide gaps in the ground. She was joined by many others who came out of their homes and just stood there and prayed that they would get the people out. Some of the people who lived near the park brought out food and drinks for the men who were working. People were drawn together and were trying to help one another and the rescuers.

Helen Nichols, a young girl, soon arrived on the scene. To her, it was clear that something terrible had happened. She recalled, "We ran right up to the edge of the park and looked down. All we could see were the workers outside. The train was in the tunnel underneath us. We were way up on the hill that put us about 80 feet above the frantic activity in the tunnel's west entrance."

Helen's father, Horace Nichols, a section foreman for the C&O, had walked out of the tunnel to get a tool just before the roof fell. For want of a tool, his life was saved, but he returned to help dig other people out. As Helen looked down from Jefferson Park, she had no idea how close a call her father had or that he was frantically working to try to save those who might still be trapped in the tunnel.

Hattie Finley, another young observer, was also on the scene at Jefferson Park. According to what she heard from bystanders, the tunnel caved in, it caught the engine and all the workmen underneath it and no one could get out. She felt the terrible gloom and became a part of the vigil. She recalled, "It was a huge crowd, it was terrible. People were excited and people stayed thinking they were going to get the people out."

Upon seeing the sunken side of Jefferson Park, many of those looking at the cave-in surely must have had disquieting thoughts about their own safety and the safety of their property. If they lived on Church Hill, they knew that this same tunnel ran through a thickly populated area and more cave-ins were possible, if not likely. Maybe the earth would cave in under their homes or businesses, killing their families and destroying their property. Could they feel safe in their own homes? Indeed, there were still people alive who could recall the earlier cave-ins when the tunnel was being constructed.

It was extremely fortunate that the tunnel had caved in under a park where there were no homes or buildings, but no one was able to guarantee that additional cave-ins might not occur; however, there were several efforts to provide assurances that everything was safe in order to avoid a panic.

Richmond's director of public works, Keith Compton, arrived on the scene and said, "It was difficult to determine anything definite, but I saw nothing to indicate that there will be any further cave-ins." But he still cautioned, "Unless care is exercised in the rescue work more of Jefferson Park will be drawn into the opening."

There was one location that remained an area of concern, and statements did not seem to alleviate this concern. Richmonders who lived in the block between Broad and Marshall and Twenty-fourth and Twenty-fifth Streets quickly recalled that in early June 1925, there had been indications of a settling of the earth above the tunnel. Their concerns were discounted by the city building inspector, Henry P. Beck, after he was assured by the C&O that the settling of the houses was not due to any weakness in the tunnel and that the concrete rings being placed in the tunnel would solve any problems. But the people living in the area could not be sure; they remained concerned.

While people watched, waited and wondered, steps were taken to protect Richmonders. The Marshall Street Viaduct, which connected Church Hill with downtown Richmond, was closed to all traffic, and streetcars were routed away from the affected area. City officials explained the reason for the closing by advising Richmonders that "the landslide from the cave-in had jarred and twisted two of the supporting columns of the viaduct; thus, causing a potential problem." Indeed, a streetcar was coming east on the viaduct when the cave-in occurred. Schoolgirls who were passengers on the streetcar saw the cave-in and started to scream. The motorman reversed the streetcar, and soon all traffic on the viaduct was stopped.

Other precautions were also taken. Jefferson School was very close to the tunnel, and some citizens felt it to be in danger of being hit by a landslide. The mayor of Richmond, J. Fulmer Bright, ordered that all children who attended the school be confined to the southern side of the street in front of the building. This was probably of little comfort to both the parents and the children when the collapsing tunnel was across the street from the school.

One citizen was extremely fortunate. Mr. Smith was standing on the crest of Jefferson Park, watching for schoolchildren from Jefferson and other schools who frequently would avoid the concrete steps to the top of Jefferson Park and walk across people's beautifully maintained lawns. His mission was to protect the lawns from the feet of wandering children. Since it was raining, Mr. Smith realized that the children would not cross the lawns, so he left the place where he was standing and returned home. Three minutes after he left, the ground on which he had been standing caved in. This time a life was spared because a man did not want to stand in the rain and get wet.

A number of other fortunate events came together to save lives. If it had not been raining, the children might have been playing on the hill in the area of the cave-in, or if it had caved in earlier, children might have been walking across Jefferson Park on their way home from school. And if the tunnel had caved in at almost any other point, many houses would have been destroyed with a possible loss of life. Providentially, the tunnel gave way under Jefferson Park, which was one of the few places in Church Hill that did not have houses built on it. And if the caved-in area had been larger, more people would have been either trapped or killed. If the tunnel had to collapse, it collapsed in the best possible place at the best possible time.

As the situation at the cave-in became clearer, the general offices of the Chesapeake and Ohio Railway issued the following statement to the media:

> *Engineers engaged in recent work at the mouth of the tunnel announced early this morning* [October 3] *that they are engaged in the sinking of a shaft from…* [Jefferson Park] *in order to reach Engineer Mason at the earliest possible time. All efforts are being centered today in the effort to rescue Mason and one laborer who is reported missing. Apparently Mason and the laborer are the only ones who were in the tunnel and not accounted for. The Church Hill Tunnel has not been in regular use for several years and the men at work yesterday were engaged in putting it into regular use.*

This report constituted a statement of what the Chesapeake and Ohio Railway knew at the moment. More information would become available in the hours, days and weeks ahead.

While people were looking and reports were being issued, more rescue workers arrived on the scene to accelerate the rescue operation. To provide support for the rescue effort, members of the Richmond Chapter of the American Red Cross arrived at the tunnel, bringing needed supplies, and they were prepared to stay through the night to make sure the rescue workers were as comfortable as possible. They also kept an ambulance on the scene in case it was needed to transport cave-in survivors or any rescue workers who might be injured.

The Red Cross joined around fifty police officers who were at the tunnel, as were an equal number of firemen. In addition, a work train was stationed at the western portal to carry away debris from the tunnel as soon as it was removed by the rescue workers. The C&O was putting all of its efforts and resources to find anyone who might still be trapped in the tunnel. The desperate rescue operation consisted of work on several fronts. Rescue workers were at both ends of the tunnel, with digging taking place at the western portal by 4:00 p.m. There was no digging taking place at the eastern portal because of the poisonous gas originating in the tunnel that was aggravated by smoke from the railroad torches used by the rescuers. But there were men who continued to wait there in case a rescue operation became feasible.

At the same time that work was going on at the portals, rescuers were digging a shaft down through Jefferson Park in an effort to reach the train, and a steam shovel was clawing into the side of the park. The steam shovel was removing about 60 cubic feet of dirt every hour, which was loaded into one of thirteen waiting trucks to carry it away. It was suggested that 2,500 yards would have to be removed before the locomotive was reached. Unfortunately, around 10:00 p.m. a cable broke on the steam shovel, putting it out of operation and delaying the work.

Everyone wanted news of Mason and the rest of the missing men, but the tunnel would not yield the desperately needed information. In spite of heroic efforts, no one could reach Mason through the piled-up mud, although a dozen men risked their lives trying to worm their way through the avalanche.

The Richmond Fire Department was on the scene and had the necessary equipment to assist in the rescue operation. Firemen from Truck Company no. 2 were stationed at the western entrance of the tunnel, and members of

Engine Company no. 1 were sent into the "black mouth" of the tunnel from the eastern entrance. These firefighters from Engine Company no. 1, like other rescuers, tried to use the eastern portal as a way to get to the trapped men but were powerless to accomplish anything due to the packed earth, which proved to be an immoveable mass that even trained rescuers could not move. Although they could not save anyone by going through the eastern portal, the rescue workers continued to wait to see if, by some miracle, a tattered survivor might emerge alive from the dark tunnel. Their wait would be in vain.

As people looked, watched and prayed, workers struggled all night to get to the trapped men, "believing if a temporary passage could be opened some of the men might be found alive beneath the flatcars of the train." During the night, workers at the western portal announced that they had located the engine and were still engaged in sinking a shaft from above in an effort to reach Mason at the earliest possible time. With each shovel of earth removed by hand or by machine, the workers were getting closer to the buried train, but would they get there in time to save lives?

While the rescue operations were underway, hospitals were prepared to receive those injured, but they were eventually told not to expect anymore patients. The attempt to save lives was slowly evolving into an effort to find the bodies of the missing.

While the rescuers were at work, the citizens of Richmond wanted to know why the tunnel had collapsed. Although railroad and other officials did not have all of the information required to offer a definitive report, there were a number of preliminary reports. One report was that workers had said that streams of water flowed constantly from the roof and walls of the tunnel. It was said that the vibration from Mason's locomotive probably caused the cave-in because the leaking water had weakened the tunnel and the movement of the locomotive might have been the catalyst that set the cave-in into motion.

Inspector Beck was of the opinion that the work being done to put the tunnel back into service was responsible for the cave-in. It was known that the earth through which the tunnel ran was blue marl, a treacherous substance. The railroad workers were engaged in supporting the brick-walled oval with concrete rings and were digging earth from the tunnel for that purpose. Mr. Beck's theory was that removing the earth let in water, which resulted in undermining the side walls, thus causing the cave-in.

Jefferson Park, showing the area of the collapse of the Church Hill Tunnel. *Photograph courtesy of the Virginia Historical Society.*

The *Richmond News Leader* reported: "A C&O official observed that springs of water, seeping through the treacherous red clay and blue marl deposit to soak into the joining in the masonry for more that half a century, are believed to have caused the supports of the tunnel to give way, precipitating the terrific landslide."

The truth remained that without a comprehensive analysis, the actual cause of the collapse would remain a mystery—a mystery that focused on the same soil that had caused so many problems when the tunnel was being constructed and on the vibrations caused by the locomotive.

During the days ahead, there would be a desperate effort to save or to find the bodies of those who were still held in the tunnel. The Chesapeake and Ohio Railway would not abandon them. As the day closed, people who tried to sleep could hear drilling into the night and the sounds of the steam shovel. Many people did not sleep. They could not forget the day that touched and changed so many lives.

Chapter 10

Saturday, October 3, 1925

And oh, the men's and women's moans
Did echo through the air;
Such cries were never heard before
From humans in despair
—Unknown, "The New Market Wreck"

In 1925, people relied on their newspapers and their neighbors for information since radio was still in its infancy. If Richmonders had not heard about the tunnel disaster from some person, they certainly learned about it when they opened the *Richmond Times-Dispatch* on Saturday, October 3, 1925. The headline left little doubt as to what had happened. It proclaimed: "Two Men Known to be Dead; Two Injured; Several Others Missing as Tunnel Caves In." Other news stories about the tunnel opened with these words in bold type: "Engineer Tom Mason is believed to have been buried alive when the Chesapeake and Ohio Railway Tunnel Caves in Just Below Jefferson Park; Rescue work is pressed to limit; Accumulating gasses hampering life-saving efforts." Pictures on the front page showed the broken and twisted concrete steps and the sunken face of Jefferson Park. Stories reported on the large crowds of people that had gathered at the eastern portal to help escaping workers, as well as the large number of onlookers who had gathered on Jefferson Park to watch the rescue operations taking place.

The *Richmond News Leader*, the evening paper that claimed to cover Richmond like a roof, focused on the harrowing experience of those trapped in the tunnel. There were also headlines about the trapped engineer and other missing men. A large picture of Engineer Tom Mason with his wife, Mary, and four-year-old daughter, Nellie, was featured in the paper. The picture clearly showed the chain of his railroad watch, which was a symbol of his profession. Another story added to the emotions by noting that the "wife and little daughter await news of Tom Mason. They hold to the shred of hope that perhaps he was able to crawl out of reach of the scalding steam and still lives in the dirt and debris which has seeped under the cars." Remembering the message of Ben Mosby to his wife, it was pointed out that Tom Mason was unable to send a message. A picture of Ben Mosby showed him holding a small dog. These two pictures put a human face on the tragedy. Other pictures in the evening paper showed a jagged thirty-foot hole in the surface of Jefferson Park under which the engineer was now entombed. The *Richmond News Leader* summed up the situation by stating: "The Hazardous Work of Penetrating the C&O tunnel under Church Hill is Progressing with All Haste Consistent With Safety."

The headlines told the story, but the deep cracks in the surface of Jefferson Park marked the scene of the tragedy. The C&O continued to deploy all its resources to try to save the missing engineer and laborers. But the challenge ahead was almost overwhelming, and the citizens could only wait.

Waiting is not easy. The longer you wait, the more the anxiety increases, or perhaps you adjust to the uncertainty and focus on something that might divert your attention for a brief period of time. This was the situation facing those who had a loved one trapped or missing in the tunnel. Mentally, they tried to make the rescuers speed up their work, but they could only wish, they could not act, they could not claw away the dirt. Wishing and hoping could not speed up the process. Mrs. Mason and others could only sit and listen for a knock on the door that might bring some news—be it good or bad—or they could go to the tunnel and watch the rescue efforts.

As the hours passed, over seventy-five thousand people gathered at the site of the cave-in and watched the efforts of the rescuers to free the trapped workers. Many people stayed all day and into the night transfixed by the rescue operation. This was no longer a local tragedy. People from across the nation began to learn about the collapse of the Church Hill Tunnel from stories in the *New York Times*, the *Washington Post* and other national papers. The headline in the *New York Times* was sensational. It reported: "Rail Tunnel Traps 100 as Walls Cave." The papers warned that there were fears of additional earth slides at Jefferson Park, which could halt the rescue efforts altogether.

While the papers reported the news, the rescue workers were faced with a new challenge. New slides brought many tons of earth down from the southwestern section of Jefferson Park. These slides occurred early in the morning, but the earth had started to crack around nine on the evening of the cave-in. Before midnight, the new slide had opened a gaping fissure, measuring eight to twenty inches. Officials were not surprised by the new development. They had believed that such a slide was inevitable given the soil and the earlier cave-ins.

Unfortunately, the new slide would further delay the efforts to reach those trapped in the tunnel. People were getting increasingly uneasy. For some, this new delay was seen as the end of all hope of saving the trapped railroad workers. The only possible good news was that the new slide did not endanger the rescue workers.

To make matters even worse and to increase the uncertainty and desperation, there were persistent but unconfirmed reports that many men might still be trapped and unaccounted for in the tunnel. Any noise from the tunnel was quickly interpreted as a sign that someone was still alive and that a life could be saved. Were the trapped men trying to communicate with their rescuers by hitting on the tunnel walls? Could the trapped men hear the noise of the rescuers, and were they trying to let them know that they were still alive? The railroad, however, continued to report that only the engineer and two laborers were still missing. But was this correct? Were there more? Was there some sort of coverup of the truth?

As the shaft bored deeper into Jefferson Park, heavy wooden supports had to be added to the shaft to keep it from collapsing. In addition to sinking the shaft, rescue workers continued to bolster up the western end of the tunnel with wooden braces. It was believed that this would provide a solid support from the western portal to the place where the cave-in ended.

In spite of the cave-in and the massive rescue effort, some things returned to normal. The Marshall Street Viaduct was reopened to streetcar traffic. The streetcars of the Ginter Park and Fulton Lines, as well as other lines, resumed use of the viaduct, but it still remained closed to cars and pedestrians as a safety precaution.

But like the day before, the curious and the concerned continued to watch. Some stood on Jefferson Park or under the viaduct and watched and waited for news of the men still trapped. The *Richmond Times-Dispatch* commented on those watching and waiting: "People crowded Jefferson Park bluff overlooking the scene of the C&O tunnel cave-in and tried to picture Engineer Tom Mason who was sitting at the throttle when the falling of a single brick announced the collapse of the tunnel walls that fatally injured Benjamin F. Mosby."

The crowd continued to wait, but there seemed to be a growing realization that there was little hope of saving Tom Mason because he would have been scalded like Ben Mosby, since the two men were sitting almost side by side in the locomotive cab. But the two missing laborers, Richard Lewis and H. Smith, were not in the locomotive; therefore, they might not have been scalded. These two men might have been trapped under the flatcars and avoided the crushing dirt. This thought gave rise to the hope that they might have survived the cave-in and might still be alive, waiting to be rescued.

Although the shaft went deeper and more dirt was removed, digging a shaft was not a dramatic event to those watching. In fact, there was little to see since the men were like moles and could not be seen once they went into the shaft; however, a steam shovel at full power can be quite dramatic, aggressive and far more visible.

The observers generally focused on the work of the steam shovel. The daily papers reported:

> *People moved from place to place to get a clear view of the giant steam shovel which was eating away at the blue marl and red clay that blocked the tunnel at the rate of about a truck load a minute. If people could not get a clear view of the steam shovel, they could at least hear the puffing and croaking and could see sparks flying as the giant arm scooped away the earth, whirled rapidly, and unloaded the shovel into trucks waiting to carry away the blue and red clay.*

Throughout the day, rescue efforts were also being carried out in the western portal. It was being cleaned of debris, and at night, the crowd was transfixed by the rescuers digging into the debris from the cave-in while

The interior of the Church Hill Tunnel during the rescue operation. *Photograph courtesy of the Virginia Historical Society.*

being guided by the white lights from acetylene lamps. With all of this work, people still wondered if there was really a chance to find Tom Mason and the other men. Emotions ran the gamut, from the belief that the men were dead to the hope that they were anxiously waiting to be rescued. The answer would come in the days ahead.

During the rescue effort, Tom Mason's wife and his large family were advised of the situation and the slim chance that he might still be alive. Surely they clung to the hope that a miracle might take place. The *Richmond Times-Dispatch* encouraged the belief that Tom Mason might have survived the cave-in by suggesting that "Tom Mason might be at his throttle, his burned body supported by the loose clay which had poured in under the roof of the locomotive cab. Possibly through some miracle he is alive, and he is listening to the steam shovel as it puffs and eats into the earth." And the steam shovel continued to puff, creak and groan and shovel away the dirt that trapped the railroad workers deep in the clay of Church Hill.

There were still no rescue efforts underway at the eastern portal because of the poisonous gas. No one dared to enter the gaping death chamber with gas everywhere unless they were wearing gas masks.

In addition to reporting on the current rescue efforts, the newspapers reported on the events occurring on the day of disaster. Old news coupled with new news had one persistent theme: Richmond had experienced a disaster, and hope was fading fast that survivors might be found.

Chapter 11

Sunday, October 4, 1925

With a clear block into Heaven's gate he'll put his mighty train,
And there in God's own roundhouse he will register his name.
—C.C. Meeks, "The Wreck of C and O No. 5"

Richmond was a city of churches, and many churches were close to the tunnel. The congregations could hear the sounds of the rescue efforts taking place during Sunday services. Prayers surely were offered on this Sunday for those who had been touched by the tragedy that had occurred on Friday afternoon. Praying was the one thing that most people could do under the circumstances.

The front page of the Sunday newspaper carried a notice that Benjamin Mosby's funeral would be conducted on Monday, October 5. He was the first victim of the disaster to be laid to rest. The train, Tom Mason and the rest of the unaccounted for railroad workers were still buried in the tunnel. And an unfortunate series of events suggested that the rescue operation would come too late to save anyone.

While the shovel was trying to reach the trapped workers, the newspaper reported that

> *huge, yawning cracks were opening with fearful rapidity over the entire section of Jefferson Park hill where the big steam shovel had been cutting away tons of earth. With cracks occurring, concern was expressed about*

> *the continuous use of the steam shovel. The holes in Jefferson Park were very wide and about thirty feet deep...The earth looked like a giant cake that had been broken into bits by a family of hungry urchins.*

The opening of these cracks left the rescuers no viable or safe option but to abandon the steam shovel at three thirty on Sunday afternoon. Explaining the stopping of the steam shovel, the newspaper reported, "Fears for the safety of the southwestern half of Jefferson Park hill caused the abandonment of the work of the steam shovel." The newspaper continued: "As the giant steel teeth of the mechanical excavator ate into the bowels of the hill directly toward the imprisoned locomotive, great cracks appeared in the overhanging hillside." It was also noted that further use of the shovel might endanger the greater part of the "pretty park which overlooks Shockoe Valley." The steam shovel was a dramatic means of rescue that was highly visible and whose work and progress could be easily seen. With the stopping of the steam shovel, the first shaft was augmented by two more shafts in order to continue the rescue efforts.

The public was assured that the three shafts being dug would enable the three hundred rescuers to reach the tunnel and the trapped workers as rapidly as the steam shovel. But the general feeling continued to be that the shafts would not reach the trapped men in time, and they would not be found alive. But the digging continued.

The series of three shafts were sunk into the earth above where it was thought the locomotive was buried. One shaft was dug to reach the top of the locomotive, and the other two shafts were to reach the tunnel immediately in front of and behind the locomotive. Now those who watched could see three shafts on Jefferson Park that were plunging through the earth to reach the trapped railroad men in the tunnel below.

J. Fulmer Bright, the mayor of Richmond, arrived on the scene and inspected the rescue operations. He complimented the workers and offered them the full resources of the city to assist in the rescue operation; however, the city would only act in an advisory capacity unless more help was requested by the Chesapeake and Ohio Railway. The mayor also endorsed the use of the three shafts as the quickest way to reach the trapped workers. It was further explained to the public that once the shafts reached the required depth, lateral shafts would branch off from them to reach the train. The closer the main shafts came to the train, the shorter the lateral shafts would have to be and the quicker the men would be found.

In spite of all the public statements about the use of the three shafts to reach the trapped men, the C&O leadership continued to evaluate the rescue efforts. Accordingly, officials of the C&O had a meeting at the tunnel and reaffirmed that the use of the three shafts was the best approach to the rescue. But the failure to use the steam shovel continued to concern the onlookers. In response to this concern, the C&O's superintendent, L. Allen, addressed the issue of the steam shovel and its withdrawal from use by giving an analysis of the situation. He said, "It would have been possible to assemble even more steam shovels and make a great display of frantic digging, but that the method of sinking shafts and working in from the western end of the tunnel appeared logical and sensible."

While the debate about the steam shovel's use or nonuse was taking place, the shafts were inching closer to the train as a donkey engine lifted the dirt from the shaft to the surface where the dirt and debris were dumped into large buckets to be carried away. Another donkey engine, which was capable of carrying a huge load of dirt, was also made available to the C&O by a Richmond contractor. But the work of digging the shafts was excruciatingly slow since work had to be frequently stopped in order to put heavy timbers into place to prop up the sides and prevent the shafts from caving in. In spite of the frantic efforts, the first shaft was only about twenty feet deep; it still had at least forty more feet to go before it reached the area where Mason and the other men might be found.

As the rescue efforts were taking place, an old issue resurfaced among the people in and around Richmond: were there more than three people trapped in the tunnel? This became a very real concern when a report surfaced about 4:00 p.m. that a worker had managed to crawl out from the death pit and that he had said other men were still alive in the tunnel. Obviously, this caused great excitement among the crowd and put more pressure on the rescue workers until the report was discredited. Hearing this news, the crowd returned to their somber and orderly attitude.

The behavior of the crowd, which numbered in the thousands, was quite interesting. Jim Crow laws enforced racial segregation in Richmond; however, blacks and whites mingled together as they waited for the rescue effort to yield results. They were brought together by a common wish that someone would be pulled alive from the depths of the Church Hill Tunnel, be that person black or white.

In spite of all of the news coverage and the assurances that the shafts were the best way to bring about a rescue, the public was still getting restless. The shafts seemed to be slow, and time seemed to be slipping away. People wanted a rapid rescue that was not possible under the circumstances. To respond to these concerns, the Chesapeake and Ohio officials again issued a report to update and assure the public that everything possible was being done to rescue the trapped workers. A portion of the report was as follows: "We are now engaged in locating the train and we are also rushing the work from the western portal. It will not be possible to reach the engine before tomorrow evening [October 5] if all goes as it should and the [shaft] is the quickest way in which the work can be done. The C&O is sparing no expense in the work of reaching the men." An official also put down one rumor when he stated, "There is no truth to the report that we are planning to bring in miners from West Virginia. We have a number of expert tunnel men on the job now and all the help that can be worked to advantage."

As the workers got tired of digging, they were immediately relieved by a new crew. In addition, all C&O employees were told to be ready to work at the tunnel. A switch engine remained at the western portal to pull cars of debris out of the tunnel as soon as they were filled; however, men had to fill wheelbarrows with dirt, roll them to the waiting train cars and then unload them. This operation was quite time consuming. Since the trapped train was believed to be about seventy feet inside of the tunnel, the work at the western portal was essential to the rescue effort. Like the shafts, this work was very slow since the tunnel had to be braced to avoid another cave-in whenever dirt was removed. Mrs. Mason remembered, "Whenever they removed any dirt, more dirt fell to replace it." Because of "heavy and poisonous gas," no rescue operations were taking place at the eastern portal.

The day closed with the issuance of another statement that all was being done to reach the trapped workers, and nothing would be "gained by a feverish show of activity, and that the three perpendicular shafts being bored were the wisest and most practicable way of coping with the situation."

In spite of all of the assurances and the endorsement of the shafts as the fastest rescue operation, the people of Richmond still felt there must be a better way. The thundering of the steam shovel was equated with rapid

The interior of the Church Hill Tunnel during the rescue operation. *Photograph courtesy of the Virginia Historical Society.*

work, the digging of three shafts seemed painfully slow. Although there was a frantic effort to save the trapped men, the city was overcome with a wave of despair. It was believed that the two workmen were "working in advance of the locomotive, or perhaps beside it, when the cave-in occurred" and died when the tunnel collapsed. And Tom Mason was still trapped in the cab of locomotive 231. The Lord's Day ended with little hope that a miracle would happen and that the men would be saved from the stone, cold tomb.

Chapter 12

Monday, October 5, 1925

Now you brave railroad men all take warning.
Make your peace with God don't delay.
Let him strengthen your hand on the throttle.
For it may be your last run today.
—Buddy Preston, "The Wreck on the Hunnicut Curve"

Today, the tragedy took a very pungent turn. It was reported that one of Tom Mason's sons, Ralph Mason, continued to watch and wait around the tunnel to see if his father would be rescued. The young man refused to leave, as men dug into the collapsed tunnel in an effort to reach his father. Even his mother's persistent efforts to get him to return home were of no avail. When asked, the young lad insisted that he would wait at the tunnel until his father was found safe or his father's body was recovered. Fortunately, concerned people brought him food or took him to a restaurant.

While a young man waited to see if his father was alive or dead, nearby at St. John's Episcopal Church, a funeral was being held for Benjamin Mosby. Those who knew the young fireman, who was only twenty-six years old with a wife and a daughter, filled the church. The brave fireman's concern for his family when he escaped from the tunnel captured the hearts of Richmonders. The largest contingent of those attending the funeral was railroad men, whose calling could be determined by the railroad pocket watches they carried. As the congregation remembered the brave railroad man, the distant sounds of the rescue operation could be heard like a distant echo to remind the faithful that while they were assembling to bury Ben Mosby, others were continuing to seek anyone still trapped in the tunnel.

Following the service, the mortal remains of Ben Mosby were buried in Hollywood Cemetery. There were many flowers, but one bunch of flowers was unusual. It was sent by a former Richmond railroad man who was not known by the Mosby family. A card with the flowers read: "Just a tribute from a stranger to the memory of a gallant soul; one who, injured unto death, thought not of himself, but of those entrusted to his care. Well done thou good and faithful servant." As the burial service at Hollywood concluded, the rector of St. John's intoned, "The grace of our Lord Jesus Christ, and the love of God, and the fellowship of the Holy Ghost, be with us all evermore." The mortal remains of Benjamin Mosby were lowered into the ground. Mourners standing by the fireman's grave could hear the sounds of the Chesapeake and Ohio locomotives as they pulled long trains on the tracks by the James River near the cemetery.

Meanwhile at the site of the disaster that had claimed Mosby's life, the rescue effort was painfully slow. Although no additional cracks had appeared on Jefferson Park, there was little progress. Of the three shafts being dug in an effort to rescue the trapped men, the middle one had reached a depth of thirty-three feet, and the other two shafts that were started after the steam shovel was abandoned had reached only ten feet.

There were also continued efforts to reach the men by digging into the western portal. But in spite of all of these efforts, there was no real hope that those found in the abandoned tunnel would be alive. Still no one was suggesting that the rescue efforts be abandoned, and the digging continued. Because of the rain and the fear of more cave-ins, the police made everyone leave Jefferson Park for fear the entire park might fall into the hole made by the steam shovel before its work was stopped.

Later in the day, the Virginia State Corporation Commission in a special report stated that "failure to use horizontal braces in the C&O tunnel under Church Hill, which were demanded by a minimum factor of safety, caused the tunnel to cave in." The commission further stated that "the walls were known to be defective for years." It reported that "from 50 to 75 horizontal braces were put in the tunnel several years ago for a short distance and that most of the end blocks had been removed, thereby decreasing the support for the walls."

The old Jefferson School with Marshall Street Viaduct in the foreground. *Photograph by Walter Griggs.*

The report also made a number of recommendations with regard to the rescue work:

> *First, the entire tunnel be more strongly braced.*
>
> *Second, that no further work except rescue work take place in the eastern end until all the bracing had been installed.*
>
> *Third, it is recommended that all streetcars be temporarily rerouted away from Marshall Street between Twenty-first and Twenty-third Streets because of the vibrations they are causing and the fear* [that] *another cave-in might result.*
>
> *Fourthly, that the water be pumped out of the tunnel at once.*

A little boy waited; a family buried their husband and father; the shafts seemed to be moving at a snail's pace; the state corporation commission pointed out gross deficiencies on the part of the Chesapeake and Ohio Railway; and it was reported that poisonous gas had "completely filled the death pit," which had ended any hope of survival. The depressing day ended with waiting, watching and little real progress. Maybe tomorrow would be a better day.

Chapter 13

Tuesday, October 6, 1925

Brothers keep shovelin'
Pickin' in the ground.
Brothers, keep listening
For the train that's never been found.
—Llewelyn Lewis, "The Train That Will Never Be Found"

The news of the day was the continuing efforts to rescue those still trapped in the tunnel. Some people believed that those digging into the tunnel from the western portal would be the first to reach the trapped train. That belief was based on the fact that the entire tunnel was being opened by the rescuers.

The three shafts being dug in Jefferson Park were in a parallel line. The shaft closest to the western portal was designated Shaft no.1 and was followed eastward by Shafts 2 and 3. The middle of the three shafts had reached forty-five feet, and it was estimated that the shaft had to go down an additional thirteen feet before it would hit the area of the entombed train. This shaft was progressing at the rate of one foot an hour due to the heavy nature of the dirt that had to be removed. The public was again reminded that once the shafts being dug into Jefferson Park reached the location of the train, work would progress even slower since fewer men could work in the close confines of the lateral tunnel as they snaked their way from the large shaft toward the crushed train and those still trapped. The other two shafts were also getting closer to the train, but it was again reported from various sources that there was no chance of finding anyone alive in the Church Hill Tunnel. This message was repeated on a daily basis as a means to destroy any hope on the part of families and friends that their loved ones could still be alive in the tunnel. Sometimes the cruel truth is better than fostering an unrealistic hope.

Late in the day, the diggers in the central shaft reached the tunnel floor and struck some of the caved-in tunnel's braces. Promptly, they started a lateral tunnel toward the location of the entombed train. Even though the tunnel floor was reached by one shaft, digging continued in the other two shafts. As evening came, the situation was essentially that the floor of the tunnel had been reached by the main shaft, and a lateral tunnel was inching toward the train and its crew. The only glimmer of hope to speed up the work would be if the workers could find the flatcars that had formed an escape route for many of the survivors and use these same flatcars as a makeshift tunnel to crawl up to the locomotive.

As the rescuers continued their work, the state corporation commission received the required report of the accident that was stamped as received on October 6, 1925. The document was entitled "Report of Accident Involving Injury or Death of Persons to the State Corporation Commission."

The report was as follows:

For the 2 day of December 1925 at 3:15 p.m. at Richmond, Virginia, Work extra 231 was caught in Church Hill Tunnel when a portion of the tunnel gave way resulting in the following casualties:

B.F. Mosby age 26 fatally injured

R.J. Salmon age 35 derrick engineer right hand fracture

C.S. Kelso age 25 yard helper cut and bruised about body

G.C. McFadden age 54 yard foreman right arm broken

A.G. Adams age 27 yard helper right hip bruised, right ankle sprained and bruised

Walker W. Davis age 38 laborer stomach and leg bruised

Wm. Fountain age 40 laborer right knee and back wrenched head bruised

David Carter age 40 laborer nervous shock

T.J. Mason engineer supposed to be still in tunnel.

Following the submission of this report, the C&O submitted an additional report, saying, "Chas. Green age 53 laborer hands back and chest bruised in the accident."

Somehow, words on paper do not capture the tragedy that had taken place under Church Hill.

Chapter 14

Wednesday, October 7, 1925

Many hours did they search for their comrades
Who might live in the cold, cold cave,
But they never found one who was living
Way down in their untimely grave.
—Llewelyn Lewis, "The Train That Will Never Be Found"

Today, work continued on the lateral shaft as it inched toward the trapped locomotive. To help with the work, air hammers were being used to drill through all of the debris between the workers and the train. Work was also taking place in the other two shafts. Rescue operations remained suspended at the western portal because of another cave-in, but work was taking place at the eastern portal where braces were being placed near the area of the cave-in.

Although the public was frustrated with how slow the rescue was proceeding, it must be remembered that these rescue workers were risking their lives to reach the trapped train because the stability of the tunnel was unknown. The tunnel had already claimed a number of lives. It would be foolish to risk additional lives in what was now believed to be only a search for bodies.

The only other news was that the school superintendent, Albert H. Hill, reported to parents that there was no danger to either Jefferson or Bellevue

Rescue work taking place at Jefferson Park. *Photograph courtesy of the Virginia Historical Society.*

Schools being damaged by the tunnel since neither school were above the tunnel, and they were as safe as any schools in Richmond.

Maybe tomorrow would bring some news that could end the ordeal of waiting and bring some closure to the tragedy.

Chapter 15

Thursday, October 8, 1925

Headaches and backaches and all kinds of pain
Are not apart from a railroad train.
—Wallace Saunders, "The Ballad of Casey Jones"

The news from the tunnel remained unchanged. There was a rehashing of old stories by the daily papers, but they were no longer running the tunnel rescue operation as a headline. The length of the rescue operation made it old news and forced it off the front page.

Like the previous days, the newspapers reported that digging was still in progress. It was also believed that the lateral tunnels that were running in two directions might reach the locomotive tender before the end of the day. Most of the debris being hauled to the surface and being removed was brick since the top of the tunnel was ten bricks thick. This large number of bricks made the work very slow and dangerous because the bricks had to be broken up before being removed from the shaft prior to disposal. The other two shafts were also getting closer to the trapped train.

In the absence of any hard news about the tunnel, the papers provided some conjecture of where Tom Mason might be found. It was suggested that if the engineer had gotten out of the locomotive and had run toward the western portal at the time of the cave-in, his body should be found some time today in the south ditch along which the lateral shaft was proceeding. It was difficult making news out of something as undramatic as shafts being dug into the ground with no visible changes in the landscape and no real hope of saving lives.

Chapter 16

Friday, October 9, 1925

Oh, tell her to remember,
When she is old and gray,
I kissed her cheek so tender,
Before I went away.
—Bernice Coleman, "The Dying Engineer"

And the digging continued. There was a belief that the lateral shaft, which was inching eastward from the center shaft, was very close to the tender of the buried locomotive. In addition to the work from the center shaft, the other two shafts had reached either the tracks or the top of the tunnel. Air hammers were still being used to break up the bricks. It was also reported that all of the railroad cars that were not caught in the cave-in had been removed from the tunnel, and pumps were being used to remove water from the ditches on either side of the tunnel tracks. There was nothing more to report. Would the train ever be found?

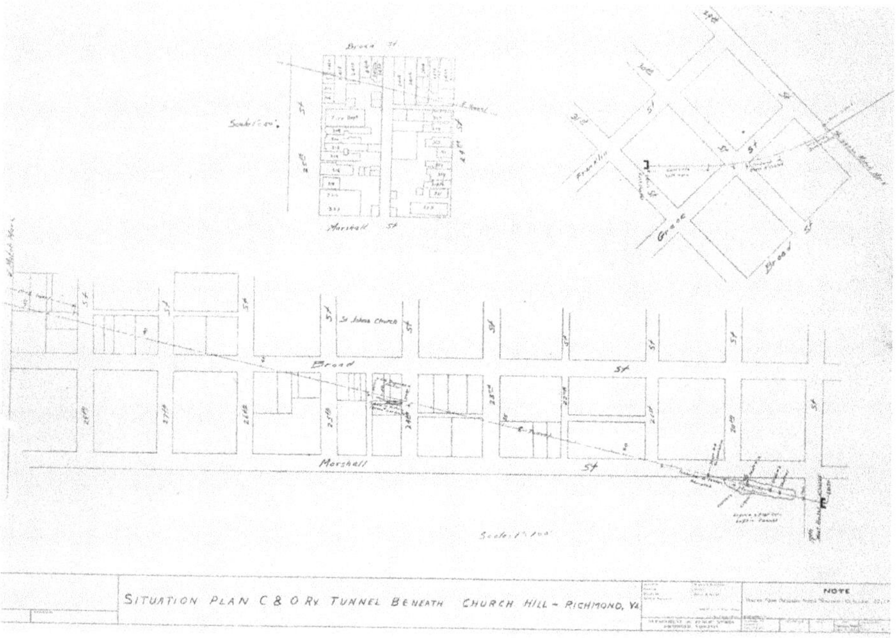

Map showing the location of the Church Hill Tunnel and the location of the shafts. *Map courtesy of the Library of Virginia.*

Chapter 17

Saturday, October 10, 1925

His time all full, no wages docked
His name on God's payroll,
And transportation through to Heaven
A free pass for his soul.
—*Unknown, engraved on the Tombstone of James E. Valentine in Hollywood Cemetery in Richmond, Virginia*

In its first edition since the cave-in, the *Richmond Planet,* the African American newspaper in Richmond, had a banner headline that read, "C and O Tunnel Cave in Here; One Hundred Men Endangered; the Engineer, Fireman and Several Colored Men Killed." The *Richmond Times-Dispatch* reported that the body of Tom Mason had been located in the tunnel.

The waiting by Tom Mason's family had come to an end. His body was found by workers in Shaft no. 3, the easternmost shaft, at 9:55 p.m. No other bodies were seen. The place in the tunnel where the rescuers came upon the locomotive was about twenty feet east of the line of Twentieth Street. Foreman Moore, in charge of Shaft no. 3, was in the shaft when, at a depth of about forty-four feet, his shovel uncovered the coupling that connected Mason's engine with a flatcar. Cutting through the floor of the flatcar, Moore slowly worked his way up to the locomotive. He must have been shocked and transfixed when the shaft of light from his electric lamp fell upon a ghastly spectacle: the body of Engineer Mason sitting in the locomotive's cab and held in place by the earth that had dropped from both sides of the collapsed tunnel into the cab. His head and shoulders were bent forward. The reverse lever of the engine had fallen in such a manner as to trap the engineer and prevent his escape. His body was in an advanced state of decomposition. The comment was made that it appeared as if Mason had been smothered to death, caught like a rat in a trap, although it is likely that he suffered the same fatal scalds from the escaping steam that had caused the death of the fireman. With great difficulty, Coroner James M. Whitfield and a *Richmond Times-Dispatch* reporter descended the narrow and tortuous steps that had been cut into the side of the shaft. Unfortunately, the coroner's foot slipped in the moist clay, and he fell. But he was not injured. He was able to grab hold of one of the jagged sides of one of the improvised steps and save himself from a fall of forty feet down the shaft. The doctor arose, smiling and declaring that he was entirely uninjured. Eventually the coroner saw the body of the deceased engineer; although his body had been found, its removal from the death cab would not be easy.

The graphic, detailed account of the body carried in the local papers must have torn at the heart of Mrs. Mason and her family. There was no more hope—Tom Mason's son could go home. But others waited to see if any more bodies would be found. The waiting and the digging continued in the quest to find more men who might have been trapped in the tunnel.

Chapter 18

Sunday, October 11, 1925

For who can speak for those who dwell
Behind the curving sky?
No man has ever lived to tell
Just what it means to die.
Swift toward life's terminal I tread;
The run seems short tonight,
God only knows what's at the end;
I hope the lamps are white.
—Cy Warman, "Will the Lights Be White"

It was time to remove Tom Mason's body. Only by using oxygen tanks and emergency tubes were the rescuers able to withstand the fetid atmosphere of the tunnel and cut the reverse lever that had pinned him in the cab. After the reverse lever was severed, the body of Tom Mason was hoisted to the surface around 9:00 p.m., about twenty-four hours after his body was located. The body was then turned over to the Bliley Funeral Establishment. Tom Mason had finished his last run for the Chesapeake and Ohio.

With the removal of the engineer's body, no real hope remained for the two black laborers who were trapped in the tunnel. Although the newspapers had focused on Mason and Mosby, it must be remembered that Richard Lewis and H. Smith were also working in the tunnel and were probably crushed to death by the cave-in. Little is known about the two missing men. Did they have plans? Did they have dreams? What were their "hopes unborn"? We will never know.

The C&O did not stop the rescue efforts with the finding of Tom Mason. They continued to dig into the tunnel in the hopes that the other bodies would be recovered and that they would not spend eternity there.

Chapter 19

Monday October 12, 1925

As you roll across the trestle, spanning Jordan's swelling tide;
You see the Union Depot into which your train will glide;
There you'll meet the Superintendent, God the Father, God the Son
With the hearty joyous plaudit, "Weary pilgrim, welcome home."
—M.E. Abbey and Charles Tillman, "Life's Railway to Heaven"

On this day, Tom Mason was buried. The service was held in Church Hill at St. Patrick's Catholic Church, which was almost on top of the tunnel that had claimed his life and across the street from St. John's Church where Ben Mosby's funeral was held. In keeping with the funeral Mass of the Catholic Church, the priest said, "O, Lord, we commend to you the soul of your servant, Thomas, that, having departed from this world, he shall live with you." Surviving him were his wife and eight children, the youngest being two years old. The church was crowded with those who came to pay their respects to the engineer, who was remembered as a very popular and respected railroad man. His body could now find eternal rest in the consecrated ground that was Mount Cavalry Cemetery in Richmond. It was reported that the railroad company would look after his family.

While Tom Mason was being buried, workers continued to look for the two laborers who were still in the tunnel. Would they ever be found?

Chapter 20

Thursday, October 15, 1925

My engine now is cold and still;
No water does my boiler fill;
My coal affords its flame no more,
My days of usefulness are o'er
—Unknown, "An Engineer's Epitaph"

The time to fix blame was at hand. Why had the tunnel collapsed? Who was responsible? A coroner's jury found that the C&O was negligent in failing to properly brace the Church Hill Tunnel while doing repair work. It was also pointed out that the C&O did not get a permit to do the work. Even though it was not legally required, proper procedure would have suggested that a permit should have been obtained. Inspector Beck of the City of Richmond testified that he had inspected the tunnel on September 25, 1925, and found there was no danger unless the foundations of the walls of the tunnel were disturbed. It was then pointed out that the foundations were probably disturbed during the construction work, which could have caused the cave-in.

Four men were dead; two of them, Richard Lewis and H. Smith, were yet to be found. Were there more men trapped in the tunnel whose names would never be known and whose bodies would never be found?

Chapter 21

Friday, October 23, 1925

Swing low, sweet chariot
Comin' for to carry me home.
—Unknown, "Swing Low, Sweet Chariot"

Although weeks had passed and workers had continued to dig into the tunnel, the bodies of the two black laborers had not been located. The C&O pledged that the searches would continue for the two missing men until their bodies were found or every inch of the tunnel has been searched.

Once the search was compete, the C&O planned to fill the tunnel with sand. Since only about two hundred feet of the tunnel had caved in, it could have been repaired and put back into service; however, the tunnel had been a source of constant trouble and was no longer essential to the operation of the C&O. By filling it with sand, the tunnel would no longer be able to trap trains and kill and injure workers. The railroad also pointed out that to remove the locomotive would require an outlay amounting to more than $30,000—certainly more than the train was worth—and such a task could be accomplished only by digging into the side of the hill and perhaps causing another disaster.

The newspaper reported: "The train which still lies buried beneath thousands of tons of clay will be packed with clay and remain under the hill until the end of time." A final eulogy for the train was recorded in the Richmond paper: "The train may not be seen again for another geological epoch when men of a new civilization discover a relic of the Twentieth Century embalmed in stone which was once the blue marl of Church Hill." And somewhere in the tunnel, there were the bodies of two men who were not found—bodies of men who were the last tragic victims of the Church Hill Tunnel.

In addition to the newspaper's eulogy for the train, a poetic tribute was written by a railroad man for his brothers in overalls who died in the tunnel. Llewellyn Lewis, who worked for fifty years on the Southern Railway as a brakeman, wrote the words of a poem within a few days of the tunnel's collapse. The music was written by Billy Pierce, and the work was published and copyrighted by the Pierce Music Publishing House in Richmond.

"The Train that Will Never be Found"

Remember the Church Hill Tunnel
Near a mile under Richmond town—
There's a story I want to tell you
Of a train that'll never be found.

On a bleak afternoon in the autumn
When the skies were overcast
A train and its crew were working
In the tunnel performing their tasks.

No one dreamed of danger
Of a death that was hoverin' near
They were happy while they were working
For the loved ones home so dear.

When all on a sudden a tremble,
A large gap in the slimy clay—
Then the earth claimed a few in its clutches
In the darkness the rest groped their way.

Many shovels and picks were diggin'
For their pals in the buried train—

Site of Lumpkin's Jail and African American Cemetery where the first dirt taken from the tunnel was dumped in 1872. *Photograph by Cara Griggs.*

Chesapeake and Ohio excursion train on the viaduct showing Richmond as it appeared in the late 1960s. *Photograph by Walter Griggs.*

But the cold slimy clay held its victims,
Soon their hopes were found in vain.

Many hours did they search for their comrades
Who might live in the cold, cold cave,
But they never found one who was living
Way down in their untimely grave.

Brothers, keep shovelin'
Pickin' in the ground.
Brothers, keep listenin'
For the train that's never been found.

Chapter 22

Remembering the Church Hill Tunnel

Oh listen to that whistle scream
Like echoes from the blue
The blood is white and spouting steam
She's on her way to doom.
—Cliff Carlisle, The Devil's Train

In 1963, I wrote the following conclusion for my thesis on the tunnel:

> *Today the Church Hill Tunnel is in a state of decay and ruin. The western portal of the tunnel under the Marshall Street Viaduct is sealed with concrete with the date, 1926, chiseled on the surface. Weeds have grown up in the area largely obscuring the ornate façade of the tunnel and the rusty railroad tracks that still run into the portal. A large masonry block stands beside the track which served as a base for signal lights when the tunnel was in use. Jefferson Park, under which the locomotive is buried, still carries the scars of the cave-in on its sides. Jefferson School, where Mayor Bright ordered all students to the south side of the building for fear of further cave-ins, is now used by the Richmond Goodwill Industries. The eastern portal under Chimborazo Park is still open and is used as a transfer track for cars being moved from the C&O to the Southern Railway.*

Almost fifty years after writing this, a lot has changed. The western portal is now in beautiful condition. The weeds, trash, old tires and debris are gone.

It is now easily accessible to visitors and is a fitting memorial to those who died on October 2, 1925. The scars on the surface of Jefferson Park remain, but the viaduct that was closed to prevent its possible collapse has been replaced by the Martin Luther King Jr. Memorial Bridge. The Goodwill building is gone, but there are many examples of urban renewal in the area that have increased the number of people who have seen the western portal of the tunnel and reflected on the events of that tragic fall day.

The eastern portal remains difficult to visit. The entire area is covered with trees, weeds and debris, and the old tracks leading to the eastern portal have been removed. With the tracks gone, the Southern Railway—now the Norfolk Southern—no longer backs cars into the tunnel. Although the Chesapeake and Ohio Railway is now part of the CSX system, its trains still cross the viaduct, enter Main Street Station and use both the Seventeenth Street and Fulton Yards.

Several events have taken place, again bringing the tunnel to the attention of the public. In 1960, Richmonders watched the dedication of C&O

Dedication of a C&O locomotive in Richmond, Virginia. *Photograph by Walter Griggs.*

Kanawa Class E4 steam locomotive at Travel Land Park. At the dedication, Governor J. Lindsay Almond captured the meaning of the steamer when he said, "Old 2732, you are not dead. In the hearts of those who love you and our kind, you will never die." This ceremony and this locomotive reminded many people of the days of steam and a tunnel that still held another locomotive, "which would never be found." I can still recall a child shouting, "Look at the choo-choo." And a lot of people looked at that big "choo-choo." Today, this powerful giant, which once ruled the rails, is on display at the Science Museum of Virginia waiting for the engineer to say, "Green Board."

Other reminders of the tunnel are the frequent cave-ins. In 1961, there was a landslide at Jefferson Park that caused the concrete steps to crumble. These landslides were not unusual and were attributed to the continued collapsing of the tunnel.

More recently, in 1996, the tunnel was featured in one of Patricia Cornwell's novels, *Cause of Death*. Cornwell wrote:

> *I stared into the black opening of a tunnel that long ago had been dug into a mountainside too soft to support it, and I moved closer until I was just inside its mouth. A wall sealed it deep inside, and whitewash on bricks glistened in my* [flash] *light. Rusting railroad spikes protruded from rotting tires and were covered with mud and scattered about were old tires and bottles.*

On October 2, 2000, the seventy-fifth anniversary of the cave-in, Bob Harrison of Harpers Ferry, West Virginia, organized a tribute to those who died in the tunnel. Mr. Harrison said, "This country was built on the premise that all people count...that individual lives and the pursuit of happiness are important." After some additional comments about the deplorable state of the tunnel, he continued, "It is time the city stopped allowing this cemetery to be vandalized because the western portal is as close to a tombstone as these men will ever get." I was quoted as saying, "No one deserves to be buried in a dump. Men who gave their lives to improve the infrastructure and flow of commerce in Richmond deserve a better final resting place." At the ceremony, a plaque with the following inscription was placed at the tunnel: "In memory of the unidentified African-Americans whose souls rest in this tunnel 75 years to this day after its collapse."

The plaque, which has now been badly mutilated, also had the names of the known dead from the disaster. Following the ceremony, those assembled at the site sang these lines together in memory of those lost in the cave-in:

Amazing Grace, how sweet the sound
That saved a wretch like me.
I once was lost but now I'm found
Was blind but now I see.

As the hymn was being sung, I recall thinking that perhaps the wandering spirits of those who died might know they had not been forgotten.

A prize-winning song written in 2008 by Russell Lawson once again told the tragic story of the Church Hill Tunnel:

"Church Hill Tunnel"

Our daddy worked for the C&O
He loved those trains and the places that he'd go
Richmond town was where we settled down
The only home we'd ever know

Twenty years he rode the lines of steel
As loader-brakeman, then as engineer
When he'd get home we'd stay up through the night
To hear his tales by candle light

Chorus:
A moon of bone shines down on the tracks
Where Church Hill Tunnel has fallen in
The C&O man said daddy's gone
And won't be comin' home again

Well, Momma told us that we ought to pray
When Mrs. Mason came around that day
The killer tunnel that ran beneath the clay
Stole her Tom and dad away

Chorus

Church Hill Tunnel claimed so many lives
The railroad sealed it so no one else would die
A locomotive engine still buried deep inside
Train whistles still make momma cry

Chorus

And won't be comin' home again

Mark Holmberg, a former newspaper columnist and now a TV reporter, was able to enter the tunnel and record his experiences in an article printed in the *Richmond Times-Dispatch* on July 5, 1998. His comments are fascinating. As Holmberg crawled into the tunnel via the eastern portal, through which Ben Mosby had escaped, he saw that the ceiling was leaking and that there were cracks in the brickwork. As Holmberg and his companions continued

Bridge abutment that was used to support a bridge leading to the Church Hill Tunnel. *Photograph by Walter Griggs.*

into the tunnel, they had to crawl over the rocks and sand that covered the floor. After "crawling about 500 feet into the tunnel, they noted that the ceiling was twisted and cracked and the men sensed they were entering the *Twilight Zone*." In order not to add to the list of those lost in the tunnel, they backed out; unlike Tom Mason, they again saw the light of day.

In the summer of 2006, H.P. "Pete" Claussen, chairman and CEO of the Gulf and Ohio Railway, planned to remove the train from the Church Hill Tunnel. His plan was to dig holes in Jefferson Park over the area where the train was located and to lower a camera to photograph the train in preparation for its removal. It was suggested by Robert G. Kelly of the University of Virginia that the locomotive would be "wrapped in a cocoon of rust and earth that has been impregnated by the decaying metal." But Kelly felt it still might be in pretty good shape, but very fragile.

On July 13, 2006, a camera was lowered into the tunnel, but only water was seen. The contractors had started pumping water out of the tunnel when it was realized that the company had not applied for street permits or submitted a water disposal plan. The City of Richmond stopped the operation for fear of causing more cave-ins, for the lack of permits and for concern for the safety of Church Hill. The expedition failed to recover the locomotive, and perhaps it is best that it be left at its final stop with some of its crew still there. But there are those who believe the train and some workers are still asserting themselves in a very unsettling way.

When I first saw the Church Hill Tunnel with my grandfather, it seemed to project a strange feeling. I felt it sending out unsettling vibes. The thought of dead men and a rusting train sealed in the earth does cause a person to have weird thoughts and nightmares. There are reports that on especially damp and dreary days with a light rain falling and fog hugging the shallows, the ghost of the work train can be seen chugging up the track near Church Hill. Reportedly, the flatcars are full of laughing workmen with their picks and shovels and a smile on every face. I wonder why they are smiling. With a little imagination, perhaps you can really see ghosts of railroad men riding on a work train, or perhaps they are carrying lanterns and looking for the train that "has never been found."

There are also many stories about strange activities in and around the tunnel. One story seems to suggest that things might really go bump in the night. A man who worked in the building next to the tunnel "reported hearing sounds coming from inside the tunnel." The sounds were of pickaxes

Picture of the west portal prior to its restoration. *Photograph courtesy of the Virginia Historical Society.*

Jefferson Park in 2011, showing damage that remains from the cave-in. *Photograph by Cara Griggs.*

"ringing on brick and rock." The man believed that those still trapped in the tunnel were trying to dig themselves out. A similar account reported the sounds of voices coming from underground. The voices were heard to scream, "Get me out!" I find these stories a bit unsettling, but I certainly would not discredit them. And I would just as soon not witness them.

Although it might be possible to ignore noises and maybe voices, you certainly cannot ignore a vampire. What is a vampire? A vampire as defined by the *Oxford English Dictionary* is a "ghost or a reanimated corpse that sucks the blood of sleeping people." Obviously, vampires are not sought out as neighbors, but there might be one lurking around Richmond as a result of the collapse of the Church Hill Tunnel. There are a couple of versions of the vampire story.

One version told of a vampire, showing jagged teeth and skin hanging from its badly burned muscular body, running from the Church Hill Tunnel when it collapsed. Seeing the vampire, a group of men chased it to Hollywood Cemetery where it disappeared into a mausoleum bearing the name of William Wortham Pool. The men who chased the vampire could not retrieve it from the mausoleum. Maybe it is best to let sleeping vampires lie!

Pool mausoleum where the vampire might reside. *Photograph by Cara Griggs.*

A second version of the story began with someone crouching over a man. Suddenly, the crouching figure got up and turned around. Horrified, people saw his bloody mouth filled with jagged teeth. They chased him, and like the other version of the story, he entered the tomb of Mr. Pool. Is there a basis for this vampire running though Richmond after the tunnel collapse? Perhaps!

It will be recalled that when the tunnel collapsed, Fireman Benjamin Mosby ran out of the eastern portal, badly burned with his skin hanging from his body. Surely he was a horrible sight, and he probably frightened those who saw him. Ben Mosby's escape is probably how the vampire story got started. As far as I know, Ben Mosby was buried in Hollywood Cemetery and does not reside in Mr. Pool's mausoleum.

Mr. Pool was a bookkeeper. Nothing has been discovered that connects him with Ben Mosby. But there have been reports of satanic activity around Pool's mausoleum, including people breaking into the tomb and tossing body parts around the area. It should be noted that vampire stories seem to be associated with a disaster, and the collapse of the Church Hill Tunnel certainly was a disaster.

Grave marker of Thomas Mason in Mount Calvary Cemetery. *Photograph by Cara Griggs.*

Grave marker of Benjamin Mosby in Hollywood Cemetery. *Photograph by Cara Griggs.*

Another story was based on the erroneous idea that the tunnel collapsed on a passenger train filled with passengers and that the passengers are still trying to get out of the train after all of these years. Apparently, if you go to the tunnel quietly and wait patiently, you can hear them banging on the tunnel walls.

In the years ahead, I suspect that more stories will emerge about the Church Hill Tunnel when spirits, ghouls, vampires and other assorted creatures of the night assert themselves. Maybe a vampire will mysteriously create a website and scare another generation. I prefer to stay with the facts of the collapse of the tunnel since there are enough interesting, historical mysteries to last for generations without becoming involved with the supernatural. In fact, there are still occasional cave-ins that remind people that there is a tunnel under Church Hill. Its restless spirit apparently will not stay still.

As I finish this story on a rainy summer night, I can hear a CSX train sounding its diesel horn at a grade crossing several miles from my house. The mournful sound of the locomotive is a reminder of that tragic day in October 1925, when brave men died in a hellhole masquerading as a tunnel. And as the sounds of the train fade away, my thoughts once again return to two men buried in the Church Hill Tunnel with "the train that will never be found."

Bibliography

Books

American Railways: The Chesapeake and Ohio Line, Late the Virginia Central Line. Reprint, Ann Arbor, MI: University of Michigan Library, 2009.

Annual Report of the Chesapeake and Ohio Railroad. N.p.: Chesapeake and Ohio Railroad, 1868–1878.

Bergman, Scott, and Sandi Bergman. *Haunted Richmond.* Charleston, SC: The History Press, 2007.

Casto, James E. *The Chesapeake and Ohio Railway.* Charleston, SC: Arcadia Publishing, 2006.

Chesson, Michael. *Richmond after the War, 1865–1890.* Richmond: Virginia State Library, 1981.

Chesterman, William Dalla. *The James River Tourist: A Brief Account of Historical Localities on James River.* N.p., n.d.

Christian, W. Asbury. *Richmond Her Past and Present.* Richmond, VA: L.H. Jenkins, 1912.

Dabney, Virginius, *Richmond: The Story of a City.* Charlottesville: University of Virginia Press, 1990.

Dorin, Patrick. *The Chesapeake and Ohio Railway.* Burbank, CA: Superior Publishing Company, 1981

Drinker, Henry S. *Tunneling, Explosive Compounds and Rock Drills.* New York: John Wiley and Sons, 1878.

Frazier, Harry. *Recollections.* Huntington, WV: Chesapeake and Ohio Railway Company, 1938.

Hoffman, Steven J. Race. *Class and Power in the Building of Richmond, 1870–1920* Jefferson, N.C.: McFarland and Company, 2004.

Lawder, J.H. *Franchisè.* Richmond, VA: Ware and Duke, 1900.

Lyle, Katie Letcher. *Scalded to Death by the Steam.* Chapel Hill, NC: Algonquin Books, 1991.

Ordinances of the Council of the City of Richmond and Certain Resolutions. Richmond, VA: William Byrd Press, 1914.

Rachleff, Peter J. *Black Labor in the South: Richmond, Virginia, 1865–1890* Philadelphia, PA: Temple University Press, 1984.

Routes, Resorts, and Resources of the Chesapeake and Ohio. N.p., n.d.

Silver, Christopher. *Twentieth Century Richmond: Planning, Politics and Race.* Knoxville: University of Tennessee, 1984.

Turner, Charles W. *Chessie's Road.* Richmond, VA: Garrett and Massie, Inc., 1956.

Whitehead, Paul. *The Recreations of a Presiding Elder.* Nashville, TN: Southern Methodist Publishing Company, 1885.

MAGAZINE ARTICLES

Ellet, Charlie. "The Church Hill Tunnel." *New Dominion Life Style* (August-September 1975).

Huger, Thomas B. "Tom Mason at the Throttle." *Virginia Cavalcade* (Autumn 1984).

James, G. Watson. "Railroad Tunnels under Richmond." *Railroad Journal* (November-December 1960).

Kollatz, Harry, Jr. "Subterranean Secrets." *Richmond Magazine* (June 1998).

Lyon, Ed. "The Church Hill Tunnel Disaster—Recalled Again." *Chesapeake and Ohio Historical Magazine* (June 1989).

———. "Photo." *Chesapeake and Ohio Historical Magazine* (April 1989).

Namiot, Bill. "The Church Hill Tunnel Disaster." *Old Dominion (Richmond) Highball* (June-July 1992).

Science: A Weekly Record of Scientific Progress (November 1880).

Tarrant, Julian. "The Story of the Church Hill Tunnel." *Old Dominion (Richmond) Highball* (September 1982).

NEWSPAPERS

Charleston Courier, January 28, 1873.

Daily Dispatch (Richmond, VA), February 2, 1872; May 22, 1872; January 15, 1873; October 3, 1873; October 8, 1873; November 26, 1873; December 2, 1873; February 12, 1884; June 2, 1889; December 20, 1895; January 2, 1891; June 23, 1891.

Daily Phoenix (Columbia S.C.), December 4, 1873.

Daily Press (Newport News, VA), October 24, 1899.

Daily State Journal (Alexandria, VA), November 17, 1871; November 21, 1871; December 23, 1871; February 1, 1872; February 2, 1872; May 7, 1872; May 13, 1872; May 14, 1872; May 28, 1872; September 23, 1872; September 23, 1872; October 26, 1872; December 14, 1872; December 26, 1872; January 15, 1873; January 22, 1873; January 29, 1873: January 27, 1873; March 5, 1873; March 24, 1873; April 9, 1873; April 19, 1873; April 25, 1873; May 14, 1873; June 9, 1873; July 10, 1873; September 17, 1873; October 17, 1873; November 19, 1873;November 26, 1873; December 11, 1873; December 13, 1873.

National Republican, June 2, 1873; June 29, 1873; December 2, 1873.

New York Times, September 10, 1883; April 20, 1892; April 21, 1892.

Richmond Dispatch, January 15, 1873; October 1, 1873; November 26, 1873; December 20, 1885; July 2, 1889; March 31, 1891; June 23, 1891; August 18, 1898; January 20, 1900; February 23, 1890; March 11, 1890; October 25, 1890; January 2, 1891; June 23, 1891; October 3, 1894; December 20, 1895; August 18, 1898; January 20, 1900; February 21, 1900; June 21, 1900; August 25, 1900; September 11, 1900; February 1,1901; February 28, 1901; April 28, 1901; June 21, 1901; April 28, 1901; May 24, 1901; May 25, 1901; June 6, 1901; June 27, 1901; November 28, 1901; August 16, 1902; May 10, 1904.

Richmond News Leader, October 3, 1925; October 4, 1925; October 5, 1925; October 6, 1925; October 7, 1925; October 8, 1925; October 9, 1925; October 10, 1925; October 11, 1925; October 12, 1925; October 13, 1925; October 14, 1925; October 15, 1925; October 16, 1925; October 23, 1925; April 8, 1952; October 10, 1985.

Richmond Planet, October 10, 1925.

Richmond Times-Dispatch, July 31, 1903; September 11, 1904; October 3, 1925; October 4, 1925; October 5, 1925; October 6, 1925; October 7, 1925; October 8, 1925; October 9, 1925; October 10, 1925; October 11, 1925; October 12, 1925; October 13, 1925; October 14, 1925; October 15, 1925; October 16, 1925; October 17, 1925; October 23, 1925; November 11, 1935; May 8, 1949; March 21, 1971; December 1, 1981; April 15, 1987; July 5, 1998; January 20, 2000; October 1, 2000; January 1, 2001; June 23, 2001; August 9, 2006; October 25, 2006.

Richmond Whig, February 3, 1873.

Times (Richmond, VA), October 6, 1899; June 3, 1891; February 21, 1900; January 13, 1901; May 25, 1901; June 11, 1901; June 25, 1901; February 9, 1902; March 12, 1902; April 23, 1912; November 27, 1901; November 28, 1901.

Washington Post, October 3, 1925.

Voice (Richmond, VA), October 11, 2000.

MISCELLANEOUS MATERIALS

City of Huntington. "The First Train," http://www.cityofhuntington.com/pages/history9.asp.

Cogito: A Journal of Where I came From. "Helen Nichols and the Church Hill Tunnel Collapse," http://nodelad.blogspot.com/2009/08/helen-and-church-hill-tunnel-collapse.html.

Richmond Presents. "Haunted Richmond: A Handful of Richmond Ghosts, Part 2," http://richmondvapresents.com/haunted-richmond-a-handful-of-Richmond-ghosts.

Virginia Black History Archives, Church Hill Oral History Project. Virginia Commonwealth University, http://www.library.vcu.edu/jbc/speccoll/vbha/school/school.html.

Virginia Historical Society. "Richmond's Buried Train," http://www.vahistorical.org/news/richmondtunnel.htm.

Western portal in 2011. *Photograph by Cara Griggs.*

About the Author

Photo by Jason Chan.

Walter S. Griggs Jr. is a professor at Virginia Commonwealth University in Richmond, Virginia. He holds a master's degree from the University of Richmond Graduate School, a juris doctorate from the University of Richmond School of Law and a doctorate from the College of William and Mary in Virginia. Griggs has authored or coauthored five books on subjects ranging from the Civil War to moose, as well as numerous academic articles. For thirty years, he has written a local history column for the *Richmond Guide*. He and his wife, Frances, live in Richmond, Virginia, and they have a daughter, Cara.

www.ingramcontent.com/pod-product-compliance
Lightning Source LLC
Chambersburg PA
CBHW060812100426
42813CB00004B/1041
9781540206114